Success on the Job
for
Developing Young Heroes

Success on the Job
for
Developing Young Heroes

Written By: Darlise Yvette Henderson

Doc Publishing

Success on the Job
for
Developing Young Heroes

Written by Darlise Yvette Henderson

First Printing: 2023

ISBN: 978-1-7358559-1-2

Doc Publishing
P.O. Box 7503
New Castle, PA 16107

www.docpublishing.org

Dedication

To Dionna and Ja'Ir, and
all **D**eveloping **Y**oung **H**EROES!

Acknowledgements

Thanks to the Almighty, and my Lord and Savior Jesus Christ, for blessing me with the gift of writing.

Love and honor to my parents, the late Herman and Clyone Cecelia Collins-Henderson.

Special thanks to my children Dionna and Ja'lr Rice for believing in me and telling me to write.

To my Henderson, Collins, Francis, Seegars and Rice FAMILY for always supporting and believing in The Mouse, I love you all!

Thank you to my cousin Myra Morgan for her inspiration and introducing me to Doc Publishing...thank you Juliann G. Mangino, Ed.D.

Thank you to my cousin Melva Morgan, my proofreader/editor.

Love and appreciation to my brother Marvin Seegars and Rochelle (Shelley) Carter for always listening to me whenever I called to say, "Hey, do you want to hear what I wrote?"

Special thanks to Marvin's friend, 'Boston Bob' for saying he wanted a copy of my book, and he was looking forward to reading my material.

I am grateful for the spiritual support and continuous prayers from the Silas First Baptist Church of Severna Park, Maryland; Pastor Jesse Eugene Young and First Lady Gwendolyn Young.

Prayers from Minister Dee and Howard Smith, Ms. Jeanette Brown, Ms. Maxine Murphy, Mrs. Wilma Offer, Ms. Margie Sampe, and Mr. Andrew Williams (Usher President).

A very special thanks to Reverend Dr. Nicholas Meade for serving as co-editor.

Thanks to the late Dr. Laura Baton of Harrisburg, Pennsylvania; Mr. Eric Alander, my high school DECA (Distributive Education Clubs of America) teacher; and the following classmates from the Harrisburg High School Class of 1985, who told me to 'write my books' or 'go for it': Lisa Arp, Nicole Austin-Hillery, Esq., Lisa Boulware, Paula Eiland-Murphy, Shawn Feimster, Gina Finley, Teresa Harper, Amanda Manigualt, and Michelle Woodson (Cookie), my first friend in the 'burg.

I acknowledge the former staff from the Hershey Foods Corporation, Hershey, Pennsylvania for professionalism and support of my early civilian career.

I acknowledge my U.S. Army roommate Ms. Brenda F. Augustus, my war buddies, and comrades of the 227 General Supply Company,

Fort Campbell, Kentucky and Operations Desert Shield/Desert Storm, 1990-1991.

I acknowledge former members of the Maryland Active Guard Reserve (AGR) program: SGM (RET) Bill Sievers, MSG (RET) Reggie Alexander, SFC (RET) William (Bill) Cherneski, SFC (RET) Tracey L. Driver, and SSG William Stallworth. Special thanks to SFC (RET) Rhoshon Lockhart and SFC (RET) Dana Sykes.

I appreciate the support and prayers from Reverend Jocelyn Barbee of Harrisburg, Pennsylvania. Thank you to author Jamilah Londan, Jaquay Williams, Paula E. Jackson, M. Div; Michele V. Mitchell; Fiordaliza "Ana" White, and all of the writers' workshop team from Harrisburg, Pennsylvania.

Thanks to inspirational authors, Mr. and Mrs. Anthony S. Waldren, #starvinartist / the Graphic Design team for the book cover.

Much appreciation and gratitude to everyone who said they would purchase my books.

To God be the glory.

Table of Contents

Introduction

CONGRATULATIONS! You have taken a major step towards receiving success on the job by reading this book. Working class people who employ hard may become a team lead, manager, or supervisor in a fair environment.

A team lead is normally the person responsible for managing a specific project or assignment(s) with limited decision-making authority. Decisions that may impact the organization are normally routed through proper channels or a manager. The team lead may conduct meetings or assign tasks as required, or function as the supervisor when given the authority to do so. This person may be responsible for the technical or operational side of an organization and should have leadership skills as related to interpersonal interaction.

Managers strive for perfection within the office and aim for a productive operational flow. A manager's job is to command an office, a project, or a team of some sort. Managers may approve absences or leave requests based on the requirements of the job. A good manager focuses on the company goal and vision. He or she may have the authority to recommend time off and award staff members accordingly. A competent manager should know and be able to perform the job of each person in the office.

A supervisor may also manage while ensuring organizational rules are followed. This is the person in charge of pretty much everything.

He or she is the boss. The supervisor is ultimately responsible for the success or failure of the office or company. Granted this person may or may not get fired if the mission fails, but he or she answers to someone for mishaps on the job. The supervisor may have seniority on the job, or an educational background that qualifies him or her to have such authority. He or she not necessarily does the work but should know the basic tasks of each person's performance plan or job assignment.

Throughout this book I will use the terms manager, supervisor or team lead interchangeably while addressing leadership. Regardless of your title, achieving a favorable outcome is normally the goal in the workplace. When people care about making money and doing what is right in the world, they normally do their best, they read, learn, and perform.

This book provides work-related tips in the areas of basic employee requirements, management, character development, and public speaking. The material covered is based on actual occurrences while the tips are derived from human experience, graduate level education and military training.

If you need a refresher regarding success on the job, or if you are new to the workforce, prepare yourself to receive information to benefit your career and life in general. Here are a few things to consider before you delve into this book that you may have experienced or witnessed:

- Mental, physical, or verbal abuse on the job

- The workplace was a place of relaxation

- Accusations of being toxic or misrepresented based on falsehoods or jealousy

- Compliments regarding performance

- Laboring with people who arrive late to work and often request or simply leave early

- A mentor modeling good leadership skills

- A dysfunctional environment with unethical leaders and liars who have done everything within their power to convince others that *YOU* have a problem

- Receipt of a time off or cash award

- Someone totally unqualified in a senior position

- Someone overqualified for a position

- Fear of speaking in front of crowds or a small audience

- Receipt of a negative unwarranted performance appraisal

- Improved office morale

- Received a rejection letter

- A desire to hurt someone on the job, or just wanted the person to 'go away'

- Engage in an inappropriate relationship for a variety of reasons

- Finding your soulmate on the job

- Sexual harassment, gender, age, or racial discrimination

- Someone asking you to teach a class on communication, or your area of expertise

Can you relate to any of the above points? Whether you can or not, you will find something of interest as you read. Grab a highlighter and a writing utensil to take notes, answer a few questions, and prepare to develop yourself for the better. Now, sit back, take a deep breath, and enjoy this journey.

PART ONE

Employee Tips from A to Z

An employee is a person who works for someone or a company, paid a salary, or is paid by the hour for their performance. Unpaid employees are volunteers or people who give of their time without asking for anything in return. Some volunteers are truly passionate about a cause and honestly do not mind working for free. You also have free laborers forced to perform community service due to various reasons.

Entrepreneurs own their own business and are considered employees of their firm. People in this category organize and operate by their own rules. They are risk-takers, they start a company at their own expense, or have others invest in their dream. Some use an aggressive approach towards business success. Others wait for an opportunity to hit them. There are also conservative people who step out on faith to start up an organization, but they do not throw all their eggs in one basket. Innovators make money through inventions.

Regardless of why you work, everything you do in life should be done in decency and in good order. The following tips will help you become successful on the job and should leave you with a stress-free work life.

Describe yourself as an employee, or the one you would like to become.

_____

_____

_____

A

Arrive on time.

It matters not if you are a new employee or have worked for three or four years, you should always arrive to work on time. Upon arrival, greet your co-workers with a warm smile, a gracious hello, or "good morning." In a virtual environment, you can place something friendly in the chat to render the greeting of the day.

You may or may not have a lot in common with your co-workers, but for whatever reason you are still there. So, for the time being, play and work nicely. When meetings are scheduled, try to be seated and ready at least ten minutes prior. If virtual, log in early and wait for the host to arrive or join in. Be familiar with the virtual app, as some programs prevent you from logging in until the host begins. Try not to have people waiting on you before anything can start.

How can you improve your punctuality?

_____

_____

_____

B

Be aware of gossipers.

Some people report to work with their problems in their pockets or on their faces. Your place of employment should not be the place for drama - especially personal. Trust me when I say, people will discuss your issues more than you - if you make it their business by bringing it to work. When people leave the job, some will leave the job at the office. Others will post your business on social media or discuss it during happy hour. Please keep your personal life separate from work and try not to get romantically involved with anyone on-the-job.

Fraternization places you in an uncompromising position. If you are solicited in such a way that is uncomfortable you should immediately address the case with the person and ask him or her to stop. Make note of the situation by indicating what happened, when it occurred, and how you handled any unwanted advances.

If you plan to tell someone what occurred, prepare yourself for what may come next, depending on who you tell in the office. A manager or supervisor should use the protocols in place for such incidents. However, if the perpetrator is your boss, please report it to higher authority or contact the police if you want to file criminal charges.

I witnessed a situation where the senior leader married and had children by someone who previously worked in his section. Unbeknownst to him, he was the subject of office ridicule and continuous gossip, especially from his peers. For whatever reason, he thought it was a clever idea to brief the entire company on sexual harassment and inappropriate behavior as if no one knew of the salacious conduct between him and his girlfriend at the time they worked together.

Workplace gossip is a recipe for ruin. It is hurtful and unethical. Avoid listening to it and engaging in negative talk. Positive language and professional communication are your best options.

Explain various forms of gossip and inappropriate behavior?

_____

_____

_____

C

Communication.

Communicate directly with your supervisor when you encounter circumstances that may cause you to be late for work. You can inform your co-workers of your absence as a courtesy, but more importantly you want to let your boss know of your expected absence or arrival time. You should always speak directly with the person who has the authority to approve or excuse your absences; it is your responsibility to take care and maintain a secure position within the workplace.

Communicating with everyone except the boss is not a good idea. If you do not like the person in charge, you probably should look for a new job. However, while you are there, give the senior officials their respect for being in the position. You do not have to like folks, but you 'should' respect people because that is what you would want from them, and a small amount of respect goes a long way.

Maintain open and honest communication with everyone on the job. Personalities may clash, but tactful communication should always be used. Tact is the tone used when you speak and say certain words. During my twenty plus years in the military and in the civilian sector, I

11

concluded that a lot of people either do not know the meaning of tact or they just do not care how words come out of their mouth.

I worked for a young supervisor who asked for my leadership guidance; it was good to know that she self-identified her weakness. I did not have a problem mentoring her because, after all, that is what I do with the Developing Young HEROES (DYH) youth and young adult leadership program. In the beginning she listened to whatever I had to say, but overtime, I guess she grew tired of my advice. Constructive criticism was something with which she struggled, as she often took offense to it and would say her feelings were hurt. However, she never considered the feelings of others whenever she spewed negative words.

This supervisor knew her job but led with her emotions, often getting upset whenever someone from the team asked a question about her decisions. The supervisor did not know how to lead, supervise, or manage. Her leadership skills lacked in written and oral communication. I started to think that she did not like people, or she could have had a behavioral health concern considering all the emotional highs and lows that occurred with her way of addressing others.

As an employee, if you are ever in this situation, please maintain professionalism and convey your words wisely when speaking to senior staff. If you do not know what to say, you can always write it out and have someone else read it to ensure you are effective in making your intended point. You can practice your words on video or share with a friend to get feedback. My point here is for you to use common-sense when communicating.

During times when there is a need for passionate language, just think before opening your mouth. I must close this section by saying effective communication is essential, but sometimes silence is golden in that being quiet is safer than speaking.

How can you maintain a positive flow of communication?

_____

_____

_____

D

Do what is right.

People work for different reasons. Whatever your reason, "Blessed are they who observe justice, who do righteousness at all times" (Psalm 106:3). Doing what is right implies that you care about your work. It also demonstrates your level of maturity, and responsibility while defining your work ethic.

Here is an effortless way to look at work ethic. Imagine that you are a restaurant chef and a customer comes in who orders a burger. Your job is to prepare the burger as requested, be it well done or medium rare. On this day, you as the chef are in a sour mood. Is that reason to take your anger out on the food? Fix the burger as if you are feeding yourself. Remember, do unto others as you would have them do to you.

If you were the owner of a company, would you want employees taking shortcuts to complete a task? If your name is going to be on the finished product, make it a beautiful outcome. If you feel as if you could care less, you probably should seek a different line of work.

Doing what is right means showing up and showing out. Let your actions prove that you deserve that promotion because you do your job, you arrive on-time and you communicate in a professional manner without gossip or envy.

Always work with determination and drive. Settling for second best is out of the equation. Be the perfectionist when it comes to completing tasks, but do not beat yourself up if you make a mistake. Your work reflects you, so do your job and do it well.

How can you prevent yourself from slacking on the job?

_____

_____

_____

E

Educate yourself.

Employers appreciate staff members who want to learn and master new skills. If your goal is to advance on-the-job you should strive to know your boss' job. Know the mission of the company and why you are there. Share insight where areas can be improved. Keep an open mind and understand that everything you say may not be received, but at least demonstrate your interest in developing your skills and knowledge.

Today's technology allows almost anyone to learn various skills for free. With access to the internet, you can access the world wide web (www) via a computer or smartphone to begin your search for knowledge from reliable sources. If you do not have any of those resources, the free public library is available for your convenience and learning, with tutorials on how to use the web and training at the library.

Some companies will pay for your education if the courses you take are in line with a specific field. I encourage you to take advantage of free education whenever it is offered to you. Many college courses or certifications are available online. This means that you can complete your degree from the comfort of your home. Let your leadership know that you want to learn more - if you do. Receive learning as an opportunity for success and as a means for growth. Ask your manager what programs are in place for self-development. If you are maxed out with education, think about teaching others what you know.

What steps will you take to enhance your education?

_____

_____

_____

F

Flexibility.

As life happens you must remain flexible because the job must and will go on. Your boss might be in charge on Monday, but for whatever reason your happy-go-lucky boss is no longer there when you report to work the following day. So now you will have to adjust to no nonsense Noah, your new manager.

You will experience several jobs and new supervisors throughout your lifetime. Some jobs will last a few months, while others may extend beyond a few years. Stay the course and eventually you will have the job of your dreams. The late Colin Powell said, "A dream doesn't become reality through magic; it takes sweat, determination and hard work."

Keep work fun and forgive others for mistakes. Work is what you make of it, so why not enjoy it with a positive attitude. As new leaders take on their new role, you may begin seeing changes for better or for worse. This is when you must keep an open mind and stay flexible. Flexibility is required as operational changes occur; therefore, stay focused on the mission and enjoy the ride.

How have you managed change in the workplace?

_____

_____

_____

G

Genuine.

Try your best to have genuine conversations. Keep in mind that work is not high school or college. Act professional even if you are the youngest person in the office. Certainly, if you are an older staff member, leave the disciplinarian within you at home. The world is not perfect, but kindness is free. Use gentle words even when you feel otherwise.

Address members by their correct title or name. Avoid unapproved nicknames or calling someone 'sweetie' or 'hun.' If you are uncertain about a name's pronunciation, it is best to ask to avoid a mistake or offense.

Smiles come without charge so give them freely. A little trick I use is to jokingly tell someone not to smile; the result is usually a chuckle or giggle. Know your audience before you do this because this technique can backfire.

A genuine personality shines bright and is an excellent character trait to have. Most mature adults can detect disingenuous habits right off the bat. Keep your personality real. Be true to yourself and to others.

List a few genuine character traits.

_____

_____

_____

H

Honesty.

Honesty is the best policy. If you make a mistake, fail to complete a task, or even steal something from the job, own your mishap. People will respect you for your honesty. Granted, you may get disciplined or fired for the act, but at least you can walk out perhaps with an ounce of dignity for telling the truth.

Maintain honesty with your supervisor or co-workers, and always be fair. Remembering false truths is difficult, so stand clear of a lying tongue. People often forget the lies they perhaps spewed, but there are those who will remember ALL the lies you told. The best policy is an honest one.

Here are a few good quotes to live by:

- ✓ "Honesty is a very expensive gift. Don't expect it from cheap people." Warren Buffett
- ✓ "Being honest may not get you a lot of friends, but it'll always get you the right ones." John Lennon

✓ "Respect is earned. Honesty is appreciated. Trust is gained. Loyalty is returned." Unknown
✓ "The first step toward greatness is to be honest." Unknown

What does honesty mean to you?

_____

_____

_____

I

Integrity.

Integrity is the quality of being honest and having strong moral principles. In other words, you should always do what is right even when no one is around. Just because you know the boss is taking a week off to visit Family in Germany, you should do your job just as you normally would with pride and integrity.

Remember, someone is always watching you. Nowadays, cameras are everywhere. People will even record you entering the office late, and they may even post it on social media with a profound caption or emoji implying your late arrival or misconduct on the job. However, if you are a person with integrity, you do not have to worry about such shenanigans.

During the Covid-19 global pandemic, there were adults attending a special program at an institution. The participants were all clear of the Coronavirus. To keep it that way, the students were advised or directed to remain within the general location. One person decided to leave the area over the weekend to have dinner with Family and friends in an entirely different state.

The person posted pictures online of the enjoyable outing. The pictures were seen on social media and a screenshot was taken and nicely forwarded to the program advisors. The new caption under that Facebook post should have been "The Last Supper" because that was the student's last extravaganza before being expelled. This is an example of someone with no integrity.

How do you demonstrate integrity?

_____

_____

_____

J

Jokes...know your audience.

Jokes on-the-job should be clean and free of discrimination. If you leave race, sex, religion, and politics out of your conversations, you should be safe. Understandably, you may want to lighten the air in the office or online...just keep it decent. The last thing you need is to be accused of an off-color joke by someone you thought was disinterested but took offense and later reported you. It happens, so be very careful.

Unless your job entails comedy, leave the humor to professional comedians. The more time you spend at work the better you will get to know your co-workers. Before sharing a joke, know your audience to be certain you will not offend anyone. In some cases, you may learn the hard way.

I saw a guy at a hospital seated behind a counter. He appeared to be sleeping. As I approached the counter I jokingly said, WAKE UP! My tone was neither harsh nor demanding. I thought I was helping him considering he was the front desk clerk. His response, however, was not so nice. The man accused me of being racist. He stood up - and woke up might I add - and told me just because he was Asian, he could not help it if he appeared to be asleep. He insisted that he was awake.

In this situation, I had no idea if the man was joking or serious. Since he accused me of making an off-color comment, I attempted to defend myself, but my apology was ineffective. He did not want to hear what I had to say. I concluded that he was guilty of sleeping on the job and used his ethnicity to defend why his eyes were closed.

Take a moment to reflect on jokes on the job.

_____

_____

_____

K

Knowledge-based performance.

Knowledge-based performance relies on what you know to complete a job. Your resume should be truthful though some people will get hired based on who they know instead of what they know. You certainly want to sell yourself on paper, but going too far and making yourself sound as if you are an expert in all areas may fail you in the long run.

Once a position is offered, be true with yourself and ask yourself if you can really handle what is about to come your way. Work struggles may ensue if you accept a position based on misrepresentation or even just to receive a lucrative salary. You may get placed in a position of power, but this can serve as a lesson or a learning experience.

Having knowledge of a task is one thing, but having technical expertise is another. I applied for a specific job at least ten times. Repeatedly, I was referred to the hiring officials, yet I was never called for an interview so I decided to take a course that would place me one step closer to getting that job. I ultimately landed an interview. I was not selected. I later asked members of the hiring panel what my weakness was, considering I have a master's degree, completed the certification training, and had some experience in the field. They wanted someone with the technical expertise and insight. I had the knowledge, but not the hands-on experience for what the job required.

When you do not get the job that you think you are supposed to have, do not worry. God has something bigger and better in store for you. Those are the words that my Family and friends kept telling me, and they were right. The Lord eventually blessed me with a position based directly on my knowledge, skills, and education. To God be the glory.

Jot down notes for updating your resume.

_____

_____

_____

L

Love it or leave it.

If you dread going to work, begin looking for something more positive that will provide you with the resources you need to survive. Work should be interesting and gratifying, considering most people over the age of twenty-five spend at least eight-and-a-half hours a day working full-time according to the Bureau of Labor and Statistics.

However, before you leave a job, consider your budget and monthly bills. If you plan to rely on public assistance or unemployment, you must consider if those services will be available to you.

Think about the following questions. Do you have another job lined up? Are you financially stable to quit a job without the need for another source of income? Do you have enough savings to survive?

You do not necessarily have to love your job, but it should not feel like a mundane chore. If you are working hard for your money and you do not care about anything else, get your coins and carry on.

What steps have you taken to sustain a life of financial stability?

_____

_____

_____

M

Motivation.

What motivates you? Is money your motivator? What about peace of mind or good health? Whatever moves you in life to achieve the results or success you desire you must begin with a goal. For example, if money is your motivator and you want to save a certain amount of funds, you should identify how you will do it by starting with the intended result.

Recognize your strengths and weaknesses through self-assessments or peer-reviews. Accept constructive criticism and discern when negative comments are belittling rather than valuable. Envious people will do everything they can to degrade you when they see your dedication to a cause.

Know the obstacles or threats that could prevent you from accomplishing your objective and identify the opportunities that will lead you to success. An obstacle or threat could be another person or their position. You might have personal matters that may interfere with your professional growth. This is where management skills come into place. You should plan and organize accordingly, while mentally preparing yourself for potential setbacks. Nonetheless, ***set the goal,***

feed the soul, make the move, and complete the mission! Once you accomplish your mission - repeat the steps with a new more challenging goal.

Here are some thought-provoking quotes:

✓ "Success isn't about how much money you make. It's about the difference you make in people's lives." Michelle Obama

✓ "Too many people spend money they earned…to buy things they don't want…to impress people that they don't like." Will Rogers

✓ "Most people are prisoners, thinking only about the future or living in the past. They are not in the present, and the present is where everything begins." Carlos Santana

The time to get motivated is now! Mitigate potential risks and stop making excuses. Quit unpleasant habits, and do not blame others for anything. Take responsibility for your life and release the victim card. You got this!

What motivates you to accomplish your mission?

_____

_____

_____

N

Neat and orderly.

One might think the person with an orderly desk does not have enough to do or perhaps the person is a neat freak. A clean desk can also send the message of complete organization. An organized desk can reduce stress and prevent you from searching for documents all the while increasing productivity. Keep your area free of junk and clutter. When possible, avoid eating or drinking at your desk because spills occur, and food items usually leave crumbs which opens the door to ants or other pesty critters that could end up dead in your desk drawer.

Keep pictures of loved ones on display to a minimum. Someone once told me that a decorated office or cubicle with personal affects is a sign of a person that does not plan to progress beyond that position. Now, that comment may be true for our more seasoned employees waiting to retire. However, as an entry level worker, a few inspirational Family pictures to remind you of your purpose should suffice.

Noting that an entire display case or shelves with pictures of your Family can be a bit much unless you work in photography or a frame shop. An office is a place of duty; it is not your home. I understand the concept of "Family first," but professionalism is always paramount. As you display your loved ones, please ensure that they are appropriately dressed. I worked with a guy who thought it was okay to post a half nude picture of his wife on his cubicle wall. She had on a skimpy bathing suit that exposed a lot of flesh. He said she was a model. His wife was beautiful, but the photo was totally inappropriate for the office.

Another guy had a large mural of his children covering the wall in his office. I guess he felt the need to decorate his office the way he saw fit; *I just thought it was overkill.* Then there was the female with teddy bears and baby pictures everywhere. Her cubicle resembled a daycare center. Maybe I am old fashioned and the days of KISS ('keep it simple sweetie') are gone. Nevertheless, how you organize your workstation is your choice, whatever you decide, just keep it neat and orderly.

List a few neat and orderly key points to remember.

_____

_____

_____

O

Open your mind.

Having an open mind is a positive trait, requires a non-judgmental thought process and critical thinking skills. People with closed minds are more inclined to conduct themselves unethically. They are often involved with discriminatory behavior. The Civil Service Reform Act of 1978 makes it illegal to discriminate against people based on race, color, national origin, religion, sex, age, or disability.

Today there are many organizations with diversity and inclusion laws in place. People should be treated equally and fairly, but as you may or may not know, this is not the case. Some people may not understand this. They see things as normal or okay. They do not believe there are issues in the world, they only see things from a closed mind perspective.

Working with such people is challenging, particularly when statements such as "what is the big deal," are made when an unarmed Black American man is gunned down by a police officer after being pulled over. I have even heard people in the workplace comment negatively about the LGBTQ+ community immediately following mandatory diversity training.

Impartiality keeps everyone aware of what to expect from each other. Speak up and when in doubt have a one-on-one conversation to avoid putting anyone on the spot. People will disagree with your viewpoint and that is okay. Just know that being receptive to individuality will help you remain objective. No two people are the same, and although we all will receive a paycheck for our performance on the job, no one should be degraded while working to maintain a living.

How has diversity and inclusion impacted change in your life?

_____

_____

_____

P

Produce results.

Proactivity and productivity yield results. Serve as a go-getter. Get the required knowledge for your position and continue to excel. Even when you think you know it all, keep learning and present yourself in a humble manner. Let your co-worker's shine. If you find you need to correct your boss or another employee, do so in private.

Use caution when correcting your supervisor. Some people will not appreciate corrective feedback—while others will thank you for it. I was in a position with a young entry level supervisor who asked for my leadership guidance. Over time, I can only guess she felt threatened by my assistance and existence. I often received countless praise from leaders in other departments for my performance and professionalism. However, my supervisor began shooting down my suggestions in front of the internal department. Note: it is a serious problem if your supervisor doesn't respect you as a team player and discounts your every word. I felt her actions were out of line because she asked me to help her. I did not want her job; I only wanted everyone to be productive. Her way of doing things was often counterproductive. She acquired

results, but it was always at the expense of her team's peace of mind. No one should have to work in a toxic and stressful environment especially when the pay does not warrant the weight.

Being overworked and underpaid is never good, but if you are ever in that situation, just make the best of it until you can change your career field. Continue to produce results and try to make light of the setting. This can be done when you have the support and understanding from co-workers, Family, and friends. Working for a supervisor who is only concerned with getting the work done will hinder your happiness, your health, and your performance.

Proactive people are forward thinkers. They tend to forecast what could happen and they implement parameters to mitigate risk when necessary. Thinking ahead can prevent unsafe acts and it can also place you ahead of your counterparts when increased productivity is the goal.

What are your thoughts on productivity and results?

_____

_____

_____

Q

Quality work.

Quality work gets the promotion and the raise. If you intend not to do your best, why work? Wasting time is a waste of time. Time is something you cannot reverse or get back; once it is gone, it is gone. If you do not have the aspiration to do your job correct initially, when will you have time to do it over? Take pride in your trade and thank God that you are employed.

If you must turn in an incomplete assignment, be sure to label it as a draft or a working copy of your material. Remember, the work you do reflects your character. Quality work is error-free, measurable with factual data, and is completed on time. It satisfies everyone involved including yourself because you have either met or exceeded an expectation. The quality of your work is indicative of your responsibility and the passion you have for what you do.

Have you ever watched a movie with an evil villain, and at the end of the movie you hated the character? If so, this is because the actor performed in a manner that was so believable your emotions got involved. That, my friend is high quality performance acting that is worthy of an Academy Award. This is what I want you to do:

produce work that is exemplary and deserving of praise. Do not worry if you fail to receive positive feedback, as long as *YOU* know you gave it your all, that is what matters.

Why is quality work important?

R

Rest and relaxation.

A little rest and relaxation (R&R) hurts no one. Rest is essential to keep yourself refreshed and healthy. Giving your body time to relax on the beach or your happy place will allow you to reset your mind from the stressors of life.

Health and wellness go hand in hand. Other forms of fitness include yoga, which involves body stretching and deep breathing techniques. Meditation and Reiki can also reset your mental health. Reiki is a touchless form of energy healing and vigor for the mind and body; it is an ancient Japanese technique, used to reduce stress.

The word Reiki is derived from two Japanese words. Rei and Ki. Rei (pronounced ray) is defined as a Higher Power, and the meaning of Ki (pronounced key) is 'life force energy.' With the two words combined you have spiritually guided energy.

Demanding work pays off, but some jobs come with a lot of pressure. When stressors arise and you need a breather, take off and relax, revive, and renew your mind. Take a vacation, get some rest at home, or spend the night at a charming hotel with room service. Pamper

yourself with sunshine and fresh air. Exercise is always beneficial, so why not go for a walk.

How do you relax when you are stressed?

_____

_____

_____

S

Safety.

Safety is everyone's job. From safeguarding the information in your workplace to preventing hazards, employees should secure personal information and report unsafe acts to their supervisor. Treat the company you work for as if it is your own personal business.

Protect valuables when you go to work by placing items in a locked drawer or file cabinet. Unfortunately, bad people manage to find their way in the workplace, and if you are not careful you could end up in a negative situation. Some co-workers seek to get whatever they can at the expense of their employers.

Consider this example. Employee A is the assistant manager for a retail shoe store and holds the responsibility of managing the store's inventory. Unfortunately, the assistant manager is a thief. She steals a pair of sneakers and attempts to get away with it by adjusting the inventory log. When the senior manager discovers erroneous numbers, an investigation is launched.

Employee B serves as a retail associate. Employee B is aware of the situation and advises the assistant manager to confess to the theft.

Employees A and B now become enemies as employee A threatens employee B with physical harm if she mentions anything about the theft. We now have an unsafe work environment.

There are many ways this situation can end, but the important piece to all of this is to have safety measures in place. Become familiar with occupational safety and health policies and abstain from becoming a statistic. Knowing the rules and policies for unsafe acts can play a vital role in the event of an investigation. When accidents occur, one of the first questions asked will most likely be whether safety measures were followed. Some organizations grant time off awards when there are no accidents over a period. Time off is greatly appreciated when you need a fresh start.

Other organizations conduct fire drills and have safety binders in place with guidance related to the steps you should take in the event of an emergency. A safety officer within the organization will serve as an excellent resource for preventative measures.

According to the United States Bureau of Labor and Statistics, there were over two million nonfatal injuries and illnesses within the private industry during the year 2020. In that same year there were over one million cases that involved - on average 12 days away from work. In addition to time away from work, unsafe acts contribute to a waste of business funds that are required for investigations, claims, and/or repairs. Play it safe, watch your step, and do not allow ignorance to prevail in the workplace.

How can you remain safe on the job?

_____

_____

_____

T

Take a breather.

On any given day you may feel overwhelmed, so take time to exhale and meditate. Tell yourself an affirmation such as, "Today is a good day for an amazing day." Report to work and watch what happens. Care for yourself by finding a Zen space at work to unwind and help with your self-talk.

Some people exhale through communication. They just want to get things off their chests. You may have pent-up emotion and if so, tactfully talk to a professional. Remember, tact is having a keen sense of what to do or say to maintain good relations with others and avoid offense. Watch how you respond to others when communicating. Avoid taking your anger or issues out on the innocent. Just breathe.

A breather can include stretching at your desk. You can do three sets of ten heel and toe raises. You can also do three iterations with a ten-second hold of turning your head as far left as you can. Repeat this stretch by turning to your right and holding for ten seconds.

Another stretch is to stand up with your feet shoulder width apart and your knees slightly bent (do not lock your knees), then slowly lean back with your arms straight in the air. Hold this stretch for ten seconds, relax and repeat two more times. Control your breathing with each stretch.

Getting fresh air will also reset your thought process when needed. If you cannot go outside, look for a window to stare out at nature for five seconds. Doing this will allow you to reset your brain, appreciate the wonders of life and reduce computer eye strain.

An additional at-the-desk relaxation tip involves closing your eyes, relaxing your head and shoulders, and taking in a deep breath, exhale, and repeat. On the last deep breath in, try to hold it for five seconds and give it a forceful expiration. You can also listen to inspirational music to reset your mind. Remember to tell yourself that everything will be okay.

How do you relax?

_____

_____

_____

U

Understand your position.

You are more inclined to perform better when you know what is expected of you on the job. Some organizations will have a job description for you to review. Other places just have you show up and someone trains you on the job. If you do not know what your tasks are, please ask. If you complete your tasks ahead of time, try to focus on learning a new skill or ask for additional assignments. You may need a job more challenging if your day consists of more free time than tasks.

Avoid the desire to peruse social media or take part in any personal activity on company time. Some managers view this as stealing. This also applies to continuously engaging in small talk with co-workers. Keep in mind that some people just want to get their work done and all they want to do is go home afterwards. Know when to converse and when to remain silent.

If your supervisor chooses to talk to you while you are working, just listen and keep working if you can do so. You may have plenty of work to do, and he or she may still use your time to casually share whatever is on their mind. This can be very frustrating when you are extremely busy, but you must know where you stand. Do not do anything that your wallet cannot handle. In other words, think about what could happen by ignoring the boss. Think about how you could respond; after all, you simply want to get your work done.

Knowing your position on the job will keep you out of trouble. Even if you see some co-workers doing what you know is inappropriate you should avoid the temptation to follow suit. Just because your supervisor likes to share pictures and video footage of their pets or newborn, that does not mean you should engage in this type of activity.

Some companies have share time or coffee chats where all will talk about personal events. That is the time to share your video footage. Do not follow the lead of others when they adjust the rules. You do not want to set yourself up for failure when certain policies are violated because of one's title or position. Know where you stand in your position and when to stay in your lane.

Reflect on your responsibilities.

_____

_____

_____

V

Visitors.

Visitors should be cleared with your supervisor. Consider your colleagues before you go to work sick or even think about bringing an ill child into the workplace. It matters not if baby "Amaris" just has a low-grade fever, or if little "Envee" was sent home by the babysitter because of an ear infection.

If your baby is too sick for daycare, stay at home with your child or plan for someone to babysit. Your job, even if your workplace is a daycare center, is not the place for sick people. Regardless of how adorable or cute you think your child is, there are some people totally uninterested in seeing your sick baby at work.

This tip also applies to pets. I must include this in the same section as little babies because there are some people who consider their four-legged furry creatures as official Family. So, let us not forget them. Unless your dog "Trigger" is a service dog, please keep your pet at home…and please leave the exotic birds and snakes at home too.

Children and pets should visit your workplace when it is actually bring your child or pet to work day and it is approved by your supervisor.

What problems have you encountered with visitors on the job?

_____

_____

_____

W

Weakness.

A weakness is a quality or feature regarded as a disadvantage or fault. People will tell you how great they are but struggle with identifying their deficiencies. If you simply cannot pinpoint a shortcoming or you never thought about it, you can use that as your blemish and admit that you struggle with identifying personal imperfections.

At one point in my career, I thought I was perfect, the best at everything with no gaps and no flaws. I would answer the "What is your weakness" question by saying, "I do not have any." I now know, everyone has a vice, it may not be work related, it could be something personal. Know yourself, know what makes you tick, and what upsets you.

While at work or during an interview, you do not need to share personal shortcomings such as addictions to food, social media, or shopping. The question of your weakness comes from a professional standpoint and is often related to struggles such as time management, an inability to work with a group, or maybe challenges with effective communication.

Be careful what you share because your transparency may be held against you and can interfere with progression. Some people know their faults and can tell you exactly what they are. I have since identified my own personal issues and strive to become better each day. Since we all have vulnerabilities, and most interviewers want to hear you mention at least three flaws, you can confidently answer by stating:

1. I struggle with identifying my weaknesses.

2. I view myself as a perfectionist because I take such considerable pride in my work and some people do not like that.

3. I have an issue with thinking about work during personal time.

These answers are all true. Most people do in fact struggle with identifying professional gaps and I really do not think anyone intentionally performs any type of work without pride. As for the thinking about work during personal time, we do it every day that we prepare ourselves for the daily grind.

What are your weaknesses?

_____

_____

_____

X

Xylem is a part of a plant stem.

Xylem "typically constitutes the woody element" of a plant stem. Before you decorate your cubicle or office area, you should identify who is allergic to plants or whatever irritant you may bring in the office.

Additionally, you should consider when you will have time to care for the office greenery. If you are just starting out in a new position there is no need to get comfortable, because the goal is to move up and move on.

This may sound quite simple, but flowers and ferns require water, nurturing, and photosynthesis. Other than a greenhouse, a business office is a place to work; It is not a garden, a diva den, or your man cave. There is nothing wrong with having a few plants in the office to possibly provide you with natural Zen.

However, a desk full of plants and/or wild growing pothos (devils ivy) might bother those with allergies. Consider the environment and your co-workers. Commonplace today are small succulents such as a mini cactus or a non-toxic sedum plant that requires very little care but pleases the eye. Think about having one or two in place rather than a large leaf plant or vines.

What are your thoughts regarding plants in the office?

_____

_____

_____

Y

You are promoted.

You will eventually move on to another office or location. You will not have much to move because you went to work and kept things simple. You did your job; you did not gather souvenirs and a lot of clutter for your tiny cubicle. You proved to yourself that you are an asset to the organization. You are promoted. Along with the promotion comes peace, greater satisfaction, and additional responsibility. Sometimes a promotion comes in the form of convenience. For example, relocating to a job that is closer to home may reduce your commute, save on travel expenses, and give you more stress-free time.

A promotion can also occur as a lateral transfer, which means you will receive the same pay, but there may be a change in the position or the department which you work. Almost anyone can get a job if they apply themselves but being content while you make money is what really counts. Know the employment fit for yourself.

Having peace of mind and a positive attitude can prove beneficial when stress on the job is a concern. Find what makes you happy and work towards achieving that goal. You are on your way to success. *Congratulations!*

What steps have you taken to prepare for your next move?

_____

_____

_____

Z

Zealous attitudes.

A zealous attitude will get you noticed. True passion for your position is often exuded by your output. Bosses analyze an individual's temperament, demeanor, and deliverables while advancing their team accordingly. Pretending to work hard should be reserved for a stage or movie theater.

Use these tips to become the BEST employee within your department: Chant the company motto to rev up your drive and begin your day with zeal. As you get to know your co-workers you can say things to cheer them on to increase productivity. You can also play a motivational song in the office or place a link to a song in the virtual chat to get things going.

One day, I entered a home improvement store and noticed a crowd of employees listening to a female speaking. She was giving them a mid-morning pep talk, after which I heard loud clapping and cheering. The workers were uplifted and ready to perform. As I walked throughout the store, I witnessed a zealous attitude by everyone I encountered.

Demonstrating a zealous attitude is often a positive attribute...just do not overdo it. There is something special about that person who is a bit extra on the zeal side. He or she may present as unnecessarily loud and draws attention to all things because of *his or her* passion about work or whatever.

For example, I know a New Orleans Saints fan. He is a Louisiana native but resides in Virginia and works in Maryland. His office is loaded with Saints paraphernalia. You cannot see the walls in his office because every inch of that small 10x12 room, is covered with something black and gold - from a pair of used football cleats to signed jerseys hanging from the ceiling.

He even has black and gold candy available for others to share in his enthusiasm. He often yells "Who dat? Who dat?" if you knock on his door or stand in the doorway when the door is open. "Who dat?" is the Saints NFL motto. This behavior and his office are complete distractions from the work environment, perhaps that is his goal. No one bothers him because he gets his job done. He simply exemplifies one who is overzealous.

How do you demonstrate a zealous attitude?

_____

_____

_____

PART TWO

Management Advice from A to Z

No one manages the same because God created us all unique which is why no two supervisors are alike. Distinct as we are, everyone can learn effective management. Management is the ability to plan and organize with the intent of reaching a goal. The manager should have leadership experience, along with interpersonal communication skills, and should demonstrate effective verbal communication with the ability to motivate others to accomplish a mission without breathing down someone's neck.

Take a moment to reflect on your current situation, or your expectations for the working world. Are you truly ready for employment, the corporate world or management? Did you accept a position just for the pay? Has anyone ever called you a toxic leader or do you find yourself telling others that you are not a micromanager?

A micromanager is an inefficient person who manages with *extreme* control and pays a lot of attention to *insignificant* details. He or she is counterproductive and may lack effective managerial skills, is often closed-minded, and usually responds as if their explanation is the only correct answer.

Additionally, the micromanager presents with the following traits: does not allow you to make decisions, even if you are in a leadership position; constantly request task updates, even without giving you time to react to the work recently assigned; does not delegate or share knowledge; and would like everything done yesterday. The micromanager rarely acknowledges his or her mistakes but will point out yours. Such noxious leaders disrespect you in front of others and do not really care about your dignity or your time. He or she will speak to you in a derogatory tone, is often rude, and will justify their unprofessionalism as a person who is simply direct and straightforward, while failing to realize that professionals know how to tactfully communicate.

Part two of this book addresses the fundamentals of office administration to include virtual environments, management, and authoritative conduct. Lined spaces are provided for you to take notes or for reflection. Before you begin, jot down a few expectations for which you are looking from the material you are about to read. Keep in mind if you follow these quick and straightforward tips, success will follow you.

What are your management goals as a leader?

_____

_____

_____

A

Abuse of authority.

Using your position for personal leverage or individual gain is one way a manager abuses his or her authority. Some managers take advantage of this newfound authoritarian power and do things just because they can - DO NOT BECOME THAT PERSON. Terminating someone or giving someone a deficient performance rating just because you do not like them or you want to get back at someone for whatever reason, which is often unrelated to their performance, is a complete misuse of power.

Granted, if someone is not a good fit for a position, you should have a discussion with the person to determine the root cause of any problems. Performance conversations should occur as needed, quarterly, or at least every six months. Reviewing deficiencies or inefficiencies for the first time should not happen on the day you want the person to sign their performance appraisal or evaluation.

Delaying the conversation of one's performance will only make matters worse. The employee will most likely say no one ever mentioned anything about his or her work ethic or mediocre performance. You will have to re-do the evaluation or prepare for an investigation. In some cases, an investigation may take a while, such as in the military, but it may be worth it to prove actions. Nonetheless, if managers conduct themselves with integrity and do what is right, these instances may not happen as often.

Additionally, creating a bogus paper trail on every little incident of someone's wrongdoing is blatant harassment and emotional torture on the job for anyone. Think about this: if a person or employee is so ineffective on the job, what does that tell you about the organization, the person who conducted the training, and/or the leadership within the company? Do you really have time to write up every incident or mistake? I witnessed and worked for a few people that I will not call leaders, who composed absurd write-ups such as too many dead bugs in a desk drawer or because someone said a door was left unsecured, even though the person receiving the write-up was not present during such violation.

Office morale, core values, and excellence are driven top-down. If the higher-ups do their job, they will establish time for employee training at the lowest level. A CEO or a senior official of a business is ultimately responsible for everything for which the company name stands.

People who abuse their power will usually participate in unethical acts for which they think they can escape accountability. Rather than abusing your power, humbly share tips on how you accomplished your goals to become so efficient. Find out what motivates your team or staff to perform better. Solicit anonymous feedback from your employees to identify their perception of you to help with your self-development.

How can you improve as a leader?

_____

_____

_____

B

Be conscious of how you are perceived.

Take time to role play or conduct assessments with your coworkers to see how they view you. This can enable fun in the office, promote team building, and provide insight from the eyes of others. Practice conscious discipline on the job and use others' mistakes and negative behaviors as a learning tool for what not to do. Most grownups do not take kindly to punishment; therefore, it is crucial for all people on the job to respect each other as adults even if their behavior fails to match their age.

Telling a junior staff member to do a menial task that is not a part of their job description is inappropriate. If you would not complete such a task, what makes you think someone else is interested in doing so? Tasking out work assignments should be congruent with one's title. For example, if there are official staff members assigned to do a particular job such as shredding or custodial duties, use them accordingly.

Refrain from making degrading comments to justify your request for completing low priority work such as: "this is that part of your job that reads, 'perform other duties as required.'" Show your team that you too can shred or take out the trash at the end of the day. If you have a good team, someone will most likely speak up and tell you they will take care of such tasks. Albeit unequal in rank, position, or title, your staff will likely see that you value them as a human.

Explain the steps you will make to adjust your leadership style.

_____

_____

_____

C

Consideration.

Consideration is a good watchword. A thoughtful supervisor or manager ensures that tasks are completed in a timely manner while considering the needs of the team. If you know a member of your staff has an aversion to public speaking, you probably should not give that person the task of briefing people. Steer clear of abusing your power and forcing someone to do something just because you said so.

When leaders force others to complete an uncomfortable task, the output will often display negatively. You will receive poor production from an employee with compromised dignity and little to no integrity. Consider your outcome and plan accordingly to achieve the desired results. Know your staff.

If people want to better themselves, allow them to do it as they see fit, instead of, doing it as you see fit. Remember, you are a manager not a momager or an on-the-job dad. Know your job requirements and the people you will supervise before accepting a position of leadership. Ask about the staff during the interview process.

The caveat to this tip is: if your job or position requires you to train others in a certain field to improve performance, then you have every right to enforce compliance. Again, consider the duties of your job before accepting the position.

List important perspectives toward success.

_____

_____

_____

D

Do your best.

Follow your moral beliefs when it comes to doing your best. Doing your best is a moral code and a biblical order. It is written in the Holy Bible in 1 Corinthians 14:40, "But all things should be done decently and in order." *Please refer to your specific/personal Bible to reference decency and order.*

Once you accept a management or supervisory position it is your duty to serve in a manner that is pleasing to God, your co-workers, and yourself. Do not take anything personal and do not make assumptions. Communicate openly and honestly. Use tact when communicating in person and always maintain a professional tone when communicating via email or chats. If you have any doubts about the tone of an electronic message, you should ask someone to review it before you hit send. Once an ill-composed message is sent, the damage is done, and you may have written yourself a ticket for unprofessionalism. Perception is 90% of truth even if your intentions were not meant to be negative.

Doing your best means taking pride as you strive to accomplish your assignments. If your job is to make sure office floors are clean, you should mitigate risks such as slips, falls or trip hazards for this assignment and delegate the task accordingly. As the person in charge, you can delegate the task, but ultimately the responsibility of completion falls on you. If employees are properly trained, the manager will not have to worry about trivial details of a task such as whether mop supplies are returned to storage or if the dirt and residue were rinsed from the mop.

Perhaps your job is to calculate numbers. If so, be sure to have your facts correct, even if you must ask someone to double check your work. Accuracy is important; the miniscule details may seem pointless, but they count also.

If you must tell someone to do better or their performance is lacking, you should have specifics. Telling someone "You need to do a better job" without addressing the areas upon which to improve is quite unfair. As a manager you should always look for processes for improvement and when possible, identify a mentor for members of your team.

How can you improve your work ethic?

_____

_____

_____

E

Ethics.

The way you follow rules, policies, and behave, sets the stage for your work ethic. Ethics are moral standards that coincide with integrity, demonstrated when you do what is right even when no one is looking. Good moral ethics promote positive outcomes and shape who you are, they are spoken, unspoken, and can define your future. Bad conduct and unbecoming behavior defy the natural code of ethics.

A lazy leader will do what is convenient. Great leaders follow rules and will do what is right. In this tip, simply remember to always live and work by ethical standards. When it comes to **L.I.E.S.,** stop and think about **L**oyalty, **I**ntegrity, **E**thics, and **S**elf-respect. Forget about telling lies and gossiping about your team or the higher officials. Avoid attempting to persuade others into believing lies. You should remain loyal to yourself, your staff, and the organization.

Demonstrate loyal behavior by speaking words of truth. If the truth is negative, keep it to yourself or share only with those who need to know. Always praise in public and discipline in private. Displaying your power via yelling and stomping, exhibits weakness and unprofessionalism.

Leave threats to the weather and keep your hands to yourself.

If you witness any type of misconduct or physical altercation it is best to remove yourself from the scene, contact security, and take out your camera/phone to begin recording as long as it does not provoke anyone to attack you. The corporate grave of an inept employee should be dug by the individual; there is no need to assist. Please maintain self-respect and stellar performance and serve as a manager with integrity.

What ethical standards do you currently possess?

_____

_____

_____

F

Fruit and friends.

Providing your group fresh fruit first thing in the morning can soothe the soul. That is a tongue twister, but believe me, when you provide a person with even the smallest amount of nourishment the thought usually goes a long way. Coffee works wonders as well. This interoffice act of kindness demonstrates your concern for health and wellness.

On the other hand, doughnuts and bagels prove to be beneficial for the hungry, but not for the fitness of the individual consuming such fattening products. This is something you, as a leader can do once a month or on a special occasion for your staff.

In a virtual environment you can still have this human connection time by asking your team to share a story about wellness or they can chat about a healthy food item. The point here is to connect with your team on a personal level to show them you care about their well-being.

Human connection is very important, especially during a pandemic. Some people need to know that others care for them. Remember to ask your team how they are doing or if they had a good weekend. Patiently listen to their stories and share something nice about yourself so they can know that you too are a human with emotions.

Being nice is important, but when it comes to friendship you must draw the line. Having a relationship with members of your team outside of work can pose a huge conflict of interest when you are the boss. Co-worker luncheons are fine every now and then but clarify that each must pay out of pocket - unless you have office funds to pay for staff meals.

If you treasure your job, tread lightly if going out for drinks after work, or when attending personal birthday parties, weddings, or baby showers. There are many people who may view this act of friendship as harmless but mixing business with pleasure can cause many concerns upon returning to work.

My advice is to look at this situation objectively and think about how you would handle being blackmailed, secretly labeled the office you know what, and/or accused of favoritism. Your job is to manage; if a professional relationship develops, that is great, but remain focused and think twice about being overly friendly.

What are your thoughts about friendships at work?

_____

_____

_____

G

Go to your higher power.

Surround yourself with uplifting people whenever you feel overwhelmed. Stress is inevitable. No job is free of even the least bit of tension, it can come from the outside, or you may find yourself dealing with an unexpected Family emergency or medical concern. Just remember when life happens, and you do not know what else to do - pray.

God placed you in this position for a reason or a lesson. It has nothing to do with who or what you know. If you do not already know this, you will figure this out only if God is first in your life; the rest will follow and fall into place. Choose God, or your higher power, if it is positive. God talk is great, and the good Lord wants you to have great reverence for His word.

There are some people who beg to differ and may feel indifferent about this subject. Forcing religion or spiritual beliefs on someone may be viewed as harassment. Religion is one of those subjects that should be left outside of your place of employment. Unless you work at a church or mission of some sort, keep your prayers between you and God and in private.

How has your higher power helped you?

_____

_____

_____

H

Happiness is a choice.

You accepted the position so why are you mad, mean, and/or upset? Have you ever worked with completely negative people? No matter what you have going on, do not take your anger to work, and avoid taking work home physically or mentally. Check your emotions before you enter your living room, the office, or the virtual chat room.

Discipline and consideration are words to live by. Remain calm in the face of negativity and unprofessionalism. If you practice emotional control, you have won half the battle of happiness. Try not to allow the stressors of the job get to you.

Think about this: if you win the lottery today and resign tomorrow, guess what? The job does not stop, and the next unemployed person will gladly take your position. My point is for you to do what you can on-the-job without dread. Truth be told, some organizations really do not even care about you or their staff, they just want the work done. I witnessed a supervisor telling her staff, "Quitting is an option, if you don't like your job." This is a clear example of a person in a position of power who clearly did not give a darn about her team.

Work smartly and cheerfully as if you have already won the jackpot. Build your work around your life and think of your job as the place you have to visit and support to live the lifestyle you want. We all need money to live, but what good is the money if you are unhappy? Would you rather have a generous sum of money and misery, or happiness and a substantial income? Either way, happiness starts within. Find the joy in all things and when life fails to go as planned, allow me to happily tell you everything will be okay. Things happen for a reason and sometimes we just do not know why, so when life gets you down, choose happiness and be glad you are alive to talk about it.

What impact does money have on your happiness?

_____

_____

_____

I

Identify people by their name or pronoun.

In every individual email you should always greet the receiver with his or her name, or an appropriate title. One of the sweetest sounds in the world is often one's name. Also, it does not hurt to say hello or to make a connection comment before jumping right into the email content. Connection comments are genuine phrases such as, "Hello, how are you today?", or "I hope your day is going well." This type of communication often ignites a positive exchange that the receiver usually returns.

When contacting someone with a unique name or what some may consider a masculine or feminine name – please, please, please, find out the gender or pronoun of the recipient to avoid the mistake of calling a woman 'Sir' or a man 'Ma'am.' I was called Mr. Henderson while seated alone in a lobby. I was wearing a dress. A female Tech came out and said, "Mr. Henderson!" I stood up and said, "It's Ms. Henderson." Her response was just as bad as her mistake. She replied, "Oh, well, Henderson sounds like a masculine name." She failed to apologize but acted as if her explanation was sufficient as we proceeded to walk into the next room in awkward silence.

If sending an email to a group, please ensure that you indicate if you are talking to everyone. Blurting out information is rude and can cause confusion when it is unclear as to who or what you are referencing, addressing, or if action is required on their part. Typing something as simple as 'All' or 'Everyone' can correct this type of miscommunication. Group emails should be clear in delivery and speech because some people fail to check to see if they were carbon copied (cc'd) in the email, which can cause a person to automatically respond when they probably should not have.

Virtual chats are often very informal. People may or may not address each other by name. This is okay, but when it comes to requesting an action or delegating a task, the manager must be clear by stating the message's intended recipient.

What is your takeaway from this tip?

_____

_____

_____

J

Just exercise.

Just exercise or go to a gym, not only for your health, but also because you may serve as an essential employee. Essential workers are usually in the office bright and early, particularly during an emergency such as a fourth of December snowstorm. Managers should strive for a healthy lifestyle due to the reliance others have on them.

Reliability and resilience go together. You must take care of your health and you should know your metabolic numbers and blood pressure. If you smoke or ingest tobacco products, please stop for your own good. Some folks find halitosis offensive. No one wants to smell an awful stench every time you open your mouth. Please keep your spittoon bottle or can out of sight.

As a boss you need to have optimal health by making smart decisions on-the-job and as it pertains to your lifestyle. Many organizations designate smoke areas despite stalled smoke-free workplace laws. Right now, "there are 28 states and the District of Columbia that currently have laws in place," according to a 2020 report from the American Lung Association. Do not wait for a law's approval, act now and love your lungs.

Virtual gyms are rampant nowadays. Go on social media and select a workout video. Libraries have exercise DVDs available, or you can simply have fun by making your own workout video with your cell phone. Exercise is as simple as walking up and down the steps in your house. If you live in an apartment, you can get some fresh air while you walk around the development or community. Stretch, wiggle your toes, do yard work, or any activity that requires physical movement. A body in motion stays in motion.

What can you do to improve your health?

_____

_____

_____

K

Know thy staff.

Know your employees and cognize what motivates them. Some people are always chipper and speak to everyone, and then there are those who say very little if anything at all. Become familiar with the personalities within the office and take heed to the various cultures to avoid offending anyone.

Exude a genuine concern for others by greeting them by name and knowing when to back off after initiating a greeting. Avoid personal nicknames, instead just ask what name is preferred. Remember to ask if you are pronouncing their name properly when in doubt.

A co-worker once complained that no one spoke to her. Her concern was legitimate and prompted a discussion about inclusion. Leadership determined that the person who expressed the concern was simply stirring up trouble. She was never excluded from anything; she simply chose not to engage in any small talk. Later, it was discovered that a personality conflict between co-workers existed. The female that felt excluded expressed her concern with senior leaders by making it seem as if she was intentionally left out. She never mentioned anything to the leaders about her dislike for anyone. Know when to take complaints seriously or with a grain of salt. *Know thy staff.*

Usually, when you smile at someone they smirk and might just return the grin. Managers, please smile if nothing else. Kindness goes a long way and knowing your team and their character is indispensable. Some people may find it hard to smile - it is just who they are. You can greet them with a smile, crack a joke, or you can give them some fresh fruit and they will remain stoic. So, what should you do?

Kindly address issues that interfere with the company mission or impact others, such as customer service positions. I witnessed people reporting to work reeking of alcohol or smelling like marijuana. Drugs and alcohol can alter mental health and the ability to make decisions. Some people are functional alcoholics or drug addicts and there is not much you can do about it in some cases. Depending on the type of job you have, a drug test or urinalysis may or may not be required.

However, as a leader you should address obvious concerns. Keep in mind, unless you are a psychologist, it is not your job to diagnose the emotional state of your staff. Some workers are moody, while others are outgoing. People will share what they want you to know, and they normally will appreciate you for respecting who they are. Know and respect the personalities of your team, keep calm, and stay kind.

What steps do you take if you think someone is abusing drugs or alcohol?

_____

_____

_____

L

Listen.

Some supervisors dish out orders and then ask if the task is completed shortly after they gave the assignment. Some leaders fire and forget, meaning they will give a task and then forget about it. Then there are those who will assign a task and tell you it is a priority, but they end up either completing the task without telling you, or they will forget to tell you the task is no longer required.

If your employees constantly ask, "what is the priority," it does not necessarily mean the person struggles with prioritizing. It could very well imply there are too many tasks listed as the priority. If this occurs, nothing is a priority because the assignments are all due at the same time. It may also demonstrate a dysfunction is at hand.

Get feedback from your team. Assuming your way is the best and the only way could have drawbacks, especially if you are not a part of the working group. Listen to your staff and hear what they are saying. Follow up to ensure tasks are completed. Remember to allow time to complete the assignment before asking so quickly if a project is ready for review. Give your workers a timeline or a process map so they will know when tasks are due.

Consider that all employees are different and work at various paces, which may be different from what you are used to—especially if it is a new employee just learning. Demonstrate empathy and consideration for personal lives, which may have an impact on performance.

A former co-worker was often zealous and cracked a lot of jokes at work. One day we engaged in small talk, and she confided in me that her spouse physically and verbally abused her daily. This tip is to listen, observe, and communicate with your team because you just never know what folks are going through.

Provide employee resources as needed. Give candid feedback and explain the bane of existence when necessary. Many people today want the "why" in the work. Long gone are the days of 'do this' and 'do that' without questions. I witnessed many younger staff members asking for the reasons as to why something is done a certain way. Perhaps they have a better way of doing things, or maybe they are just curious.

Whatever the reason, hear them out and give them the tools required to complete assignments—without simply saying 'because I said so.' Such statements are ignorant and demonstrate very poor leadership skills.

What can you do to let your team know that you hear them?

_____

_____

_____

M

Meetings.

Meet with your team as required. Some departments or teams meet weekly. When weekly meetings occur, you must think about the turn-around-time for actions. Will one week serve as enough time to accomplish specific tasks? If so, great! However, if you notice that missions and goals are not met within one week's time, you may need to adjust and give your staff time to work on the assignments.

Meet at a time that is convenient for everyone, not just what is best for you. Depending on your type of organization - it is best to schedule business when employees are focused. In other words, schedule important sessions during core hours such as after 9am.

Anything can happen on the way to work. Think about the employees with school-aged children as you plan your agendas. You may not have to worry about children or perhaps car trouble, but there are others who very much would appreciate this consideration.

Avoid imposing on personal time such as lunch, especially if lunch is unpaid time. Afternoon affairs should occur around 1:30pm, because it lessens the stress of having to rush their lunch periods especially if it is only thirty minutes. Trust me when I say that people will take lunch at noon, return to work by 12:30pm, eat at their desk (if permitted), and then take a smoke or a bathroom run - if not both - all before jumping back into work. Considering the personal needs of your staff is best to maintain an elevated level of work satisfaction.

End of the day arrangements are unwise because most people want to go home, they do not want to attend anything at 3pm, especially when they get off at 4pm. Granted, some people stop everything when its quitting time, but there are those who must prepare their space prior to leaving. They may need to close the office file cabinets, secure doors, vacuum or complete end-of-day tasks. Some others will use company time to handle personal business before going home. They may make phone calls or use the restroom to freshen up before leaving the office—it happens.

A lot of these employee habits were eliminated with hybrid operations in place due to the Covid-19 pandemic. I cannot say what people do at home, but many remote workers have stated that when the duty day is over, the computer goes off, unless an alternate work schedule is in place. The bottom line is to respect others' time when planning group discussions.

When daily communication is required, have a less than fifteen-minute huddle. Bypass turning a huddle into a meeting. This fifteen-minute rule may go longer if your group is larger than ten. In-person huddles should be done in a circle; no table required. Have everyone stand around, and the Team Lead or office Manager should start out with a question related to pressing issues. If there are no immediate concerns, remind the team that you are there for any support they may need.

Conduct virtual huddles the same way with the camera on or off and pose the questions of concern. Remember, a huddle is a time to briefly address urgent issues. It is not the time to introduce new topics unrelated to the business of the day.

Long details, especially those long-winded briefings without letup, are counterproductive simply because human concentration diminishes after the first 10 to 15 minutes. Events longer than 45 minutes should stop at the halfway point. Stick to the time limit. Use a timer rather than appointing someone to watch the clock because you want everyone paying attention and not clock watching. Speak with enthusiasm and please make sure your long briefing is mentally stimulating (more on speaking later in this book).

When you have extended talks, you may notice human behavior cringing to leave or unable to stay focused. Look for these signs: people getting up in the middle of your topic, sidebar conversations, and/or folks simply standing up to stretch. Have rules in place prior to starting, tell your team when a break will occur and the guidance for cell phones and note-taking. Providing your staff with etiquette guidelines should prevent most, but not all, distractions. There is always one person who will have something more important going on in life. Such persons will simply excuse themselves and walk out.

During virtual exchanges, you will notice cameras constantly going on and off for brief periods. In some cases, you may even notice pets in the background. Cluttered backgrounds and other visuals of interest can interfere with the topics at hand. Some people will focus on the distraction and not the speaker. This is when you might want to say cameras off. Some leaders like to see faces. Others just tell you to turn on the camera simply as a means of control or connection. I witnessed a few folks get upset because someone chose not to turn on their camera. If seeing the faces of your team is required to complete a job, this is understandable. However, if seeing the faces of your team is just your preference, and not so much a showstopper, just lighten up on the virtual camera requirement, focus and find out the details later.

Kindly ask everyone to mute themselves if you are unable to silence all. Having everyone on mute while one person is speaking prevents audio interference, i.e., a barking dog, or construction sounds in the background. When distractions occur, do not take offense. Simply address it when it becomes a disturbing issue. Life happens. When you notice virtual or technical challenges by more than two people you might want to take a break.

Regularly scheduled meetings should have talking points that you should stick to during the meeting. Shy away from jumping around the points of discussion and allowing members to get off track. If you happen to divert, regroup, get back on point, and introduce new points of discussion later. This *is* your planning meeting; control the session. Being organized should prevent you from having a meeting to discuss what you will talk about at the next meeting. Plan accordingly or plan to fail. If you have an assistant who knows the talking points, <u>USE</u> the assistant, and ensure he or she brings the points of discussion. Delegate tasks—not the responsibilities.

I worked in an office with a supervisor who always had random meetings to ask a few arbitrary questions. One day, I participated in seven - mind you the normal workday was only eight hours. What type of productivity do you anticipate from your team throughout the day or week when this occurs? Do you really expect any work to be done? If your workers are constantly behind closed doors with you, when are they working?

Training sessions and performance talks should be scheduled in advance; avoid pop-ups. Find out from your team what works best. Sometimes all you need is a monthly gathering. It just depends on your organization. Impromptu sessions may happen, but when they occur entirely too often it strains the productivity of the workforce, impacts morale, and may drive you to relieve your stress by writing a book about management.

I spent a great deal of time on this topic because I observed entirely too much nonsense when it comes to this subject. Time is valuable, and once it's lost you cannot get it back. As I type this section, I feel as if I am in a long meeting. I am reflecting on the people who love to hear themselves talk, they are long-winded; God forbid, you ask a question, and the talk goes on for another 37 minutes. Two hours and thirty-seven minutes later, it all ends. There was no breather and just as you are about to walk out to start a new habit of smoking, you are called back into the office for one last thing. Unbelievable!

It is understandable when senior executives attend frequent meetings because they are not the worker bees. The point here is for leaders and managers to respect each other, and the time required for people to do their jobs.

What will you adjust in this area?

_____

_____

_____

N

No!

The word "no" is often associated with negativity, harshness, and/or rejection. Do not be afraid to say "no". If you are challenged with this word, try saying "now is not a suitable time," "let's revisit this another time," or write the word "no" on a sheet of paper. If you must revisit a conversation because you did not initially say "no" when you should have, think about why you could not say the word and inform the person that after careful thought, your answer is "no." There is nothing wrong with changing your mind.

Saying "no" is important when that is what you really mean. In today's virtual environment many people use emojis, a giphy, or other characters to get their message across. However, in a professional setting you must be clear in your meaning. When working with adults you may want to prepare yourself with an explanation. Some employees are inclined to ask the question, 'why,' especially when an answer makes no clear sense at all. Have an open mind and accept the question as valid and not as an attack on your position. Saying "no" just because you have the authority to say "no," will leave your team reeling with disdain.

Say "no" when required. There is no need to play hardball with an annoying long pause or a sigh before giving an answer. If you are asked something simple such as "is it okay to leave ten minutes early", either you are going to let the person leave or not. If an assignment is incomplete - do you really think ten minutes is going to make a difference? This is something small but important to think about as you lead people. Address attendance concerns as needed.

There are some people who make it a habit of arriving late and leaving early. They consistently take leave on Monday and Friday. Granted, vacation time is earned, but if continuous absenteeism impacts the mission or the morale of others in the office, you should have a discussion with the abuser.

Before you deny someone's request, such as leaving early, you should think about your own actions. Are you leading by example? A micromanager for whom I worked seemed to be on her own schedule. She refused to lead by example; she came and went as she pleased and often justified her early departures by blaming *her* senior leader. Granted, your staff really should not check up on you, but they do look to you for guidance and some watch your behavior.

Employees might mimic your actions, if you use profanity, so too with they. If you arrive late, they will straggle into the office. The leadership sets the tone of the organization, so avoid using your position for self-gain.

If a person must leave for whatever reason, *they must leave;* that is the end of the story. It could be for personal reasons, but some people do not want to share all their personal business with you. Have conversations about such things as early departures in advance to avoid confusion. If workloads are so detrimental that taking off ten minutes early impact the mission, you might want to review operations. Ask yourself, how bad is an early departure?

If you receive repeat requests from your staff, address the issue as there could be something else going on. Work should be fun and enjoyable. Employees should not feel like they are in grade school fearing to ask permission for every little thing. Treat people as the adults they are. When the word "no" must be used, maintain professionalism, do not apologize, just assertively say "no."

Reflect on your experience when you had to say no.

_____

_____

_____

O

Opportunities.

Opportunities for success begin with an optimistic attitude and can help make your goals a reality. Believe in yourself even if others said you would never make it in life. If you want to be the best leader, you should tell yourself every day you are number one. Always take steps to better yourself. Take pride in your work, continuously learn new skill sets, and attend developmental leadership courses. It does not matter if your field of interest is film and media or massage therapy, interpersonal development is essential.

Take advantage of every opportunity to learn something even if you have maxed out with your education. Some jobs will cover the costs of tuition or self-development courses. You can also network with people in your field of interest via LinkedIn as you seek opportunities for success. Once you reach the level of power your heart desires, reach back and assist others with their climb to the top. Teach your staff what you know, and the mistakes from which you learned.

When you see your team advance and move forward within their career fields, take it as validation that you have trained those persons well. Let others shine and always mentally uplift people. If you can make a positive change in at least one person's life, you have made a difference in the world.

What opportunities are available for you?

_____

_____

_____

P

Pride.

Pride is good when you want your work to reflect your character. Doing magnificent work is gratifying, and humility goes a long way. There is no need to boast aloud about your accomplishments because bragging about how great you are is just not a good look. People will give genuine praise when they are true to themselves. One who cannot give credit where credit is due, should look within.

Some people will never say thank you or uplift you, possibly because of jealousy. Love the position you are in and demonstrate your gratitude by doing well. Include your staff when praises are given because you did not get where you are by yourself - someone helped in one way or another. Praise God or your higher power if nothing else.

Deliver kudos to your team in public. Any type of corrective action should always be done behind closed doors. I watched supervisors berate staff members in front of fellow employees due to mistakes made. Can you imagine this type of embarrassment? Leaders and anyone in a position of authority should know how to speak to others tactfully and in a way that ignites mutual

respect. Take pride in being a
manager as you consider the pride
self.

How do you recognize your team for ou
work, other than giving them a paycheck?

_____

_____

_____

Q

Quantitative.

Quantitative and quality work defines your performance and work ethic. Are you an expert in your field? Some managers make sure the quota for the day is met and they happily go home. Others exceed their expectations and *then* go home. Exceeding your quota is an excellent standard when the work is of high quality. Going above and beyond can get you the employee of the year award, or a promotion. The key is to submit error-free quality work. Allow me to share a simple example:

Employee A can process one hundred transactions in a day with ten mistakes. Thus, the laborer completed 90% of the work without error. Additional time is now required to repeat the assignment to correct the mistakes. On the other hand, employee B completes fifty transactions in a day with zero mistakes, which gives this person a standing of 100% accuracy. The quantity of employee A is higher, but the quality of employee B is better. Knowing this difference will help you identify your star performers. Then you have employee C who completes one hundred transactions with zero mistakes. Employee C is your top wage earner.

Quality work is error-free, but mistakes can occur through human error. Consistent oversights indicate it is time to reevaluate the process of the task or the Standing Operating Procedures (SOP). There could be a disconnect with the way the steps are written, or how one was trained on the assignment.

If you produce quality work, your performance will speak for itself. Continue to work hard and allow others to verbalize your greatness. Salute yourself (with your right hand) in the mirror before you leave for work or when you go home. Tell yourself at least four wonderful things about how exceptional you are, and what you will accomplish next. Thank God or your supreme power for everything you have and will continue to receive, as you watch your money, power, and respect grow.

Reflect on the quality and quantity of your work.

_____

_____

_____

R

Respect.

Respect is a two-way street. Treat your team the same way you want them to acknowledge your position. This includes bill collectors and the maintenance people who empty the trash or clean the bathrooms. We are all human, regardless of position or title. Speak to people and say their names. Let's practice, say this aloud: "Hi Heather." Now just say, "Hi." Do you hear the difference? Saying a person's name is often music to one's ears as long as the words that follow are not harsh.

Respect is the act of holding someone or something in high regard. Respect is also a courtesy rendered when you address someone by title. Know when to call someone Mr. Joseph or Ms. Candace rather than Joe or Candy. This applies to last names as well. Note, some will say their first name is fine. Others will insist on Sir or Ma'am because they are accustomed to that. Remember, you receive respect when you render this courtesy to others.

Respect should be used in every aspect of life. At no time should you, as a leader, abuse your role by disrespecting anyone no matter what, even if *you* are disrespected. Please maintain your role as a professional and do not stoop to a lower level. Remaining respectful can prevent a situation from turning physical or leading to anything more than vile words.

I worked with a female who asked me why she did not receive the same respect as one of her peers. I had no answer, because I could not speak for others, but I mentioned my observations. She was a young leader often seen sleeping in the bathroom and was often in the wrong uniform of the day. She did a lot of partying and shared her personal business with people who, in turn, shared her private information with others. She was irresponsible and very immature. This young leader eventually somewhat got her act together but struggled with equality. If you were not her friend, she often treated you unfairly. After being promoted she acted as if people were supposed to respect her regardless of her actions. In some situations, people will respect authority. In other cases, they will not, if you are viewed as unethical and unprofessional.

You should not have to demand respect, if you do your job, it is normally rendered naturally. Carry yourself in a way that automatically commands the dignity you deserve. Dress the part, perform the role, and speak the language. Demonstrate self-respect and allow your light to freely shine.

What does respect mean to you?

_____

_____

_____

Q

Quantitative.

Quantitative and quality work defines your performance and work ethic. Are you an expert in your field? Some managers make sure the quota for the day is met and they happily go home. Others exceed their expectations and *then* go home. Exceeding your quota is an excellent standard when the work is of high quality. Going above and beyond can get you the employee of the year award, or a promotion. The key is to submit error-free quality work. Allow me to share a simple example:

Employee A can process one hundred transactions in a day with ten mistakes. Thus, the laborer completed 90% of the work without error. Additional time is now required to repeat the assignment to correct the mistakes. On the other hand, employee B completes fifty transactions in a day with zero mistakes, which gives this person a standing of 100% accuracy. The quantity of employee A is higher, but the quality of employee B is better. Knowing this difference will help you identify your star performers. Then you have employee C who completes one hundred transactions with zero mistakes. Employee C is your top wage earner.

respect. Take pride in being a well-rounded manager as you consider the pride one has for self.

How do you recognize your team for outstanding work, other than giving them a paycheck?

_____

_____

_____

S

Schedule a down day.

A DONSA is an old acronym I first heard in the Army and is defined as a **D**ay **o**f **N**o **S**cheduled **A**ctivity. In other words, there are no deadlines, tasks, or assignments required for the day. Today, some organizations call this day Focus Fridays. In some agencies there is never a dull moment. However, it is imperative to allow your team time to reset and get caught up on tasks that perhaps were pushed to the backburner due to unscheduled events or unforeseen fires. A fire is considered a small important task that may come from higher-ups in administration or a situation that requires immediate action possibly from senior leaders.

Down time allows people to close out low priority assignments, address Human Resource concerns, and focus on training and self-development. This day can also serve as time to clean their workstation or office. As the person in charge of operations you can also schedule a day of fun. Incorporate an outing with some type of health and wellness. For example, participate in a company walk or a fun run. Some companies already have activities such as an organization day in place. You do not have to wait for the annual company event, you can plan quarterly outings to give your team something to which it can look forward.

Your team will normally work hard for you, will appreciate you, and may remember you on Boss's Day, which is usually mid-October. In turn, recognize your staff on Administrative or Professionals Day, which falls on the Wednesday of the last full week in April. Selfless service is a good character trait to have. Accomplish your missions but place the needs of your team ahead of your own. You need a good team so treat your staff right.

What impact will a DONSA have on your organization?

_____

_____

_____

T

Time management.

Time management is the ability to effectively schedule your day to allow for the most productivity within an expected period. For example, if you have eight hours to complete assignments you should have an idea of how long it will take to accomplish each mission and then plan accordingly. Last minute tasks are bound to happen, avoid trying to please your superiors at the expense of your staff.

When unexpected assignments are pushed down from your senior leaders at headquarters, have the courage to ask for an extension from the person requesting the unscheduled project. Explain why or state the reason you cannot complete the untimely request whether it is unreasonable, unrealistic, or due to staff shortages. However, tell the requestor when you or your team will be able to complete the job. If you have an understanding supervisor, he or she should respect your decision.

In the event you cannot get an extension, it is okay to apologize to your team, even though it is not your fault. Letting people know you understand how frustrating it can be when a last-minute request comes in demonstrates empathy.

Reward your team with time off, an extra incentive for their arduous work, or by thanking them.

When uncompromising jobs do not allow negotiating, and you are faced with this type of pressure, choose your response wisely. Consider what is important and the impact your decision will have on the organization's mission as well as your livelihood. Ask yourself, why are you working? Do you value your peace of mind or getting the job done? These are factors to consider before accepting a decision-making position.

Identify key points of time management.

_____

_____

_____

U

Unity.

Uniting your team promotes creativity while enhancing and increasing office morale. Give employees the opportunity to display their prolific abilities. For instance, someone can implement dress casual Fridays with a theme, and it does not have to always be related to sports. Perhaps you could wear red on Wednesday or have a potluck on a Tuesday. Potlucks are fun, but in pandemic situations you should limit this activity to store-bought items. Whatever you do, never bring in leftover lima beans, half a bottle of salad dressing, or anything you obviously grabbed from your kitchen 'fridge - *yes*, someone did this.

If food from home was approved for an office function, you should write out the ingredients to alert allergy prone individuals. Use foil pans and not your grandmother's favorite stoneware, no matter how much you love it, and you want to show it off, as one false step can ruin Granny Cee Cee's porcelain pan. As the boss, do not ask anyone to clean pots or dishes that do not belong to them. If you drink coffee, make your own piping hot cup of joe, or use the individual serving cups. Do not ask or expect coffee to be ready for you when you arrive at work. Those days no longer exist. We live in a self-serve society nowadays. If there is an office refrigerator that you use along with everyone else, take part in keeping it clean and clear of leftovers. A refrigerator cleaning schedule may help.

Hopefully, people will take initiative to keep break rooms neat and clean for the next person that will use the area. Be aware that some people are unwilling to participate in shared items, space, or socialization. Just leave them alone. You should not mandate anyone to participate in team building exercises especially when you are unsure of personal feelings toward such events. True introverts do not want to participate in groups of anything.

In virtual environments, you can have your team meet via video on a Monday or whatever day you choose to gather for coffee talk. As an opening icebreaker you can ask each staff member to show their favorite mug and talk about why their mug is so special. As you know, there is always one, at least one non-coffee drinker, and that is okay. Just have them share a special teacup or water jug, the type of beverage or cup does not matter, the purpose is unity.

As for the introvert, he or she may not want to turn on their camera. You can make it mandatory, or if you 'know' your team, you will understand why he or she does not want the camera on. Spend about 15 to 30 minutes, depending on your group size, uniting, and chatting about weekend events, or announcements people may want to share. This is a way to maintain harmony and that human connection in a virtual world.

Why is unity important?

_____

_____

_____

V

Virtually yours.

Working from the comfort of your home can have benefits, but keep in mind you may have to turn your camera on if officials request to see faces. Rule number one: be camera ready. Your hair, to include facial hair, should be neatly groomed. Use a pseudo background if your home setting is unbecoming or cluttered with distractions.

Keep pets quiet, and although you may love Ace the cockapoo or Shana the cat, please keep those distractions out of sight. I hate to say it, but some people are not animal lovers, and they may fear the sight of certain animals. My dear sister Renae is afraid of cats. She will tremble with fear if a cat pops up on a screen, or if she turns the page of a magazine and discovers a basket of kittens on graphic display.

Find a location in your home that does not allow your Family or house guests the opportunity to be seen or heard. I actually saw a woman walk up to kiss her husband on the forehead. I thought it was totally inappropriate considering she clearly saw that he was at work. Only God knows what the woman was thinking when she did this. Thankfully, the employee did not engage in the

117

virtual display of affection, he simply sat there. We cannot account for the actions of others, but we can ensure our setting is in place.

Refrain from defacing your organization on social media. Your language, whether in the office or at home, is the voice of the business. Make your words match your work ethic. Understand that certain things can be taken out of context by someone who may not know your humor. For example, you would not want to say, "telework is great, I'm sitting here with my feet up and booty shorts on" - *yes*, someone said that, during a new employee virtual orientation. This embarrassing statement reflected poorly on the organization.

How can you benefit from a virtual environment?

_____

_____

_____

W

Wardrobe and appearance.

If your job has a dress code, abide by it even during dress-down days. Set the example for your employees. Wear clothes that fit, and purchase items that you can mix and match to create unique styles, a button-down-the-front white dress shirt can go a long way with a bowtie. Perhaps you can wear it slightly unbuttoned with a necklace or buttoned all the way up for that pretentious look. Either way you wear it, just wear it well.

Go to work in comfortable, clean clothes. Maintain the look of a casual expert, otherwise dress professionally and according to your position. If you are an outdoor construction worker or some other blue-collar employee your appearance may consist of a company shirt, khaki pants, or even blue jeans. Whereas white collar staff members may wear a suit or something more business-like.

Clothing for the nightclub that may entice or expose body parts should be worn at the intended establishment. Have you ever heard anyone say, "the work dress code is nightclub casual"? As mature and responsible adults, we should know right from wrong. If you need a second opinion or confirmation that you look good, ask someone if your outfit is okay. Keep in mind, when you shop for clothing, most retail associates are primarily interested in your money, not so much how you look. They will tell you anything just to get the sale.

In a virtual setting, it matters not what you have on from the waist down, focus on what can be seen. Unless a relaxed or casual wear is authorized, have a suit jacket or a sweater on the back of your chair so that you can grab it at any given moment in the event you must turn your camera on. Stay ready, so that you do not have to – get ready. Have a mirror by your desk to do a quick check of the hair and face just to be on the safe side.

Use consideration when wearing cologne or perfume in the office because some people are sensitive to certain smells. Imagine how others will feel if they are offended by your flamboyant fragrance. I once worked in an office with a lady who wore strong perfume. The supervisor kindly asked her to tone down her fragrance. The lady took offense but made slight adjustments to the amount of perfume she used. However, the scent was still very pungent, and she was conveniently 'let go'. In other words, she was terminated from the job.

If you are a smoker or drink alcohol, please know—that smell is easily detected by those who do not indulge. Inhale and/or imbibe with caution. Chronic halitosis is a concern which potentially indicates other medical issues such as diabetes, oral cancer, or even a respiratory problem. See a doctor if you have abhorrent breath beyond your normal brushing routine.

I worked in an office for an older gentleman who kept tobacco dip in his cheek. My desk was planted a good twenty feet away from the department entrance. Every time he stood in my doorway to greet me and briefly touch base on current company events, I could smell a dishonorable stench coming from his mouth. I later found out he was very unhealthy.

Groom your tresses and facial hair. Check yourself in a mirror or the camera on your phone before leaving the house. I can honestly say that I left my house one day to drop my daughter off at the childcare center, and then I drove to work. I spoke to several people along the way to include greeting my supervisor with a friendly hello and good morning.

I eventually made it to my desk where I sat down, stretched my neck, exhaled, and proceeded to rub my face as if I were pushing back a layer of relief off my forehead. As I continued to glide both of my hands over my noggin, I felt the torn stocking cap that I still had on. A stocking cap is a stretchy nylon head covering that is worn to keep your hair in place usually during bedtime and in the privacy of your home. The embarrassment I felt was shared with a co-worker, but I never understood why she did not bother to mention anything to me about my makeshift durag when she first saw me.

All these tips may seem simple and common, but in my many years of working, I saw quite a bit that warrants discussion. Outfits rip, buttons pop, and a latte will stain, so if possible, have a convenient change of clothes and shoes in the event of a wardrobe malfunction on the job.

Many interesting items were worn to an office with a professional setting and were received in a less-than-welcoming manner, such as, the beautiful sleeveless sundress with the low-cut cleavage design. This outfit sent the message that implied the employee was ready for the beach. The only thing missing was her sunglasses and her sun visor.

Another most memorable outfit was worn by a young lady during a holiday party. The dress was sequined black, spaghetti straps, and fringes at the hem that ended approximately twelve inches above her patellae. This outfit also came with shiny gold stilettos; it was a sexy mini dress/outfit most appropriate for the nightclub.

The final visual I will leave you with is the cowboy who wore alligator snip toe boots, tight jeans, and a leather belt with a shiny buckle that, for whatever reason, had a capital letter D on it – even though his first, last, or middle initials did not include the letter D. Maybe he was from Dallas, *I don't know*, and as much as I wish I did not remember this, I have to say the shirt he wore was also tight and he did not mind exposing his thorax hair. While seated at his desk he kept an unlit cigar in his mouth as if he were going to light up at any given moment. This was Mr. Cowboy's casual Friday and ready for the weekend look.

Your clothing style reflects your level of professionalism. Your staff might follow your lead, but even if they do not, it is up to you to set the standard for wear and appearance. Unless you are professionally run-way dressed, no one should ever have to give you a double take when you enter the building or office because of a hideous outfit.

Why is a dress code important?

_____

_____

_____

X

Xenocurrency, scrilla, loot, or simply the almighty dollar...

However you get your money, make sure your business is legal, pay your taxes, know the laws, and serve as a resource for others. Remain honest regarding all things financial. Know the ethics for gift giving and never give your team tangible cash. Promises of an award or a bonus should be done when you know for certain the department funds are available.

Money is the root of all evil; this is proven when people accept a management position just for the riches. If you are moved by the fortune and you plan to make it as the head honcho, just make sure you are ready to take on the responsibilities that come with the job.

You want to be in a position of authority with the basic skills of interpersonal and written communication, and the technical expertise of the job. If you knowingly lack skills, develop those skills immediately so that your staff can give you the respect you deserve. Otherwise, prepare yourself for the negative impact that will follow.

I observed liars, cheaters, and thieves work their way to the top. They stop at nothing. They will walk all over you and brag about getting ahead, all the while acting as if they did nothing wrong. They are so convincing and conniving, that no one will believe you when you mention that person's wrong doings. You may even get labeled for starting trouble. My point here is to abide by a code with which you can live. What type of legacy do you want to leave once you are called home to glory? Do you even care? What is done in the dark will eventually become known.

My advice is to not allow money to define you. I once heard this statement: money changes people. When you have the funds to change your life for the better, do so. However, do not put others down as they work towards financial growth and freedom. Do not gloat because you are the supervisor and you just paid cash for a new Aston Martin.

Reaching the top of your 'A' game is the ultimate accomplishment, so long as it is not done at the expense of others. Remain on top with profound humility. As Jesse Jackson once stated, *"Never look down on anybody unless you're helping them up."*

What are your financial goals?

_____

_____

_____

Y

Your style.

You, define your leadership style. Are you a servant leader who places the needs of others before self? Perhaps you have a democratic method where you solicit advice from others. You ultimately have the final say, but you care enough to at least render the courtesy of input. Another ordinary form of managing or supervising is an autocratic approach which is 'one-way,' and the 'only way.' In this style of leadership, the person in charge makes the decisions without consideration of what staff members may think or need.

There are many ways to lead, however; the strategic or coach process may work very well when you need to develop a team. This person combines different strategies to reach a goal while constantly looking for new and improved ways of accomplishing a task. He or she teaches, listens, and challenges people with tasks to improve on their weaknesses. Strategic or coach style leaders must perform, so as not to be viewed as the ultimate micro-manager.

Whatever your technique, this one thing is true; the youth of yesteryear are the senior leaders of today, who can certainly learn a lot from our seasoned supervisors. On the other side, older managers can very well learn from our tech savvy young adults. Regardless of your age, remain on top of technology and current trends. Some managers are stuck on one way of doing things, and one style of leading, which can become stale. Venture out and vary your style of managing if you notice that what you are doing is not working. Seek good advice and use it.

Change happens overnight, so if you can afford to hop on the bandwagon of inevitable new beginnings - then do so and step out on faith. Management is not about being liked by your subordinates; it is primarily about having common sense and the ability to get the job done in the most efficient manner while maintaining a professional attitude, and demonstrating respect.

What is your leadership style?

_____

_____

_____

Z

Zzzz...

Stop sleeping on your potential and start zapping those toxic micromanaging behaviors out of your life. You are on the path of greatness because you are reading this book. Always keep this guide with you and refer to it when you find yourself slipping. Discuss points with your team so they too, can walk in strength. Share knowledge, build together, and have the confidence to train others.

A successful workforce is derived from proper training and professional leadership. You should be able to take a vacation and know the work will get done. Leave your laptop and mobile phone at home as you depart for your trip to Brazil. Now be the good manager that you tell yourself you are and get to work.

I wish you the best as you move forward in becoming a better you. Incorporate these tips in your life and success will follow. I hope you took notes or honed-in on the letters that stood out to you. The bottom line to having Success on the job for all Developing Young Heroes is to treat people the way you want to be treated, have the ability to identify your shortcomings, and the courage to correct them.

What tips stood out to you?

_____

_____

_____

PART THREE

Character Development

A person's character is developed by morals, actions, and values. People will judge you by your words, attire, and the decisions you make in life and on the job. The image you portray should match your foundation. Think about how you live and perform at work. Are you sending mixed signals at work or home? Do you define yourself by the position you maintain at work? Does your conduct identify who you are? Are you able to answer this question: who are you?

Developing your character requires discipline and the courage to do the hard right over an easy wrong. Be a HERO on the job and live by high moral standards. Respect from others is derived from how you present yourself. Keep God First (KGF) or do so with your higher power, honor who you are, and people will respond accordingly - it is that simple. The tips in this section will help develop who you are or who you want to become.

Who are you?

_____

_____

_____

C

Conduct.

The Serenity Prayer: *"God grant me the serenity to accept the things I cannot change, the courage to change the things I can, and the wisdom to know the difference."*

Your conduct in public and in private may vary slightly. At work you are in a position of accountability and responsibility. You are required to treat others with dignity and respect. You must maintain a professional mindset in all aspects of your work ethic. People watch how you behave, respond, and react. Do so accordingly.

Outside of the workplace, in most cases, you are free to act however you see fit. This freedom of conduct comes with a price when you belong to certain organizations. There are certain things you just should not do, such as speak negatively about your employer or bring any type of shame or disgrace upon your firm. As a member of the police force, you would not want the news headlines to state something such as: OFF DUTY POLICE OFFICER ARRESTED FOR DOMESTIC VIOLENCE.

Whether you work for the federal government, or a restaurant, how you conduct yourself speaks loudly about who you are. Cell phone cameras are everywhere. The last thing you need is a viral video of yourself doing something wrong, immoral, or derogatory. Live a life free of stress and public ridicule.

Keep your personal life private. Stay focused on the job and remember your role in the workplace. You are there to accomplish a mission, make money to provide for yourself or Family, and then go home.

Describe good conduct in your own words.

_____

_____

_____

H

Help others succeed.

Demonstrate who you are by setting the example for others to follow. If you are a person with high moral principles, you will be viewed in a positive light. This trait encourages others to follow right-minded standards and become great leaders on the job or in life. Allow folks to learn and progress from your assistance.

Know when to help but remain mindful and avoid hindering others' potential by overstepping your guidance. Do just enough to get folks started by teaching people how to accomplish tasks. Some people are challenged with speaking up and will let you walk all over them. Do not force yourself on others; just let it be known that you are available.

How can you help others?

_____

_____

A

Always stand with a solid presence.

Always stand with a solid presence. Whenever you enter an area, ensure your posture is upright and your gaze is attentive. Your demeanor speaks for itself, stay alert, walk with a strong backbone, a positive sense of purpose and assurance even if you suffer from fear of the unknown.

Onlookers perceive and only know what you tell them. Give them a show of conviction. Stand straight and look over the heads of everyone in the room. Doing this little trick will shift your mind into believing you tower over everyone. This is a mental play on your brain, that will give you the feeling of power in height, at least it did for me. My height is average for a woman as I am about five foot and under four inches tall. I have no complaints about my height but feeling as if I am the tallest person in a room or taller than everyone walking down a street, psychologically makes me feel grand.

Standing with a solid presence is demonstrated by not slumping your shoulders forward, as you present with profound courage and tenacity. Present as if you oversee everything and appear as if you are the boss that you strive to become, if not already. Have a solid presence and command the room as if you own it.

What can you do to improve your posture and presence?

_____

_____

_____

R

Resilience.

Resiliency is demonstrated by how well you take care of yourself during difficult times. It is the ability to bounce back from a letdown. When you make self-care a priority your body will take care of you as you age. Rest when you must, receive routine physical exams, and exercise regularly. You are never too old to go for a walk or to take in some sunshine.

Practice mindfulness to reduce or remove stress. Nothing in life is perfect, but you can find the good in all journeys with a healthy mindset. Resilient people know their strengths and weaknesses. They know when to seek help from their support group. They are quick to recover from setbacks or negative situations.

A person who lacks resilience might suffer in silence. He or she probably will not tell anyone what bothers them. Depression may sink in. Unhealthy habits such as overeating or abusing drugs and alcohol might arise. Finances may become a problem and this downward spiral may impact work and Family.

Tell friends to check on you if they notice something strange about your behavior. Be true to yourself and know when to communicate with someone with whom you have difficulties.

We all face challenges, be it death of a loved one, having to move, or any change that affects your normal state of peace and happiness. Do not allow negative situations define your well-being. Identify your issues, seek help, and keep living. Focus on the good even when you think you cannot. Be grateful that you are alive and able to share your story.

"For his anger is but for a moment, and his favor is for a lifetime. Weeping may tarry for the night, but joy comes with the morning" (Psalm) 30:5.

How can you become more resilient?

_____

_____

_____

A

Adaptable.

You must learn how to adapt to revisions in life and demonstrate the ability to identify shifts in critical elements of a situation. Success occurs with a nondiscriminatory mind, and the ability to see the good in unique and new developments. You should view change as an opportunity for growth and learning.

A makeover can make you or break you; it is up to you to decide how you want to proceed with changes. Receive modifications as a challenge to become better. You may encounter anxiety with a new job or situation, but will you allow the newness of diversity, hinder you from being the HERO that you are?

Stress will occur; the key is to manage the stress without allowing it to handle you. You are in control of your life; therefore, have accountability for your actions and the way you respond to situations. Do not expect everything to be peaches and cream or sausage and gravy. Sometimes food will burn, what will you do? Will you eat it, throw it away, or make a new dish? The point here is to not allow negative situations to overcome your happiness. This too, shall pass, and ye shall adapt and overcome.

What are your thoughts on adapting to change?

_____

_____

_____

C

Critical thinking.

Critical thinkers ask questions; solicit feedback from others when searching for a feasible and realistic outcome. Thinking outside of the box promotes creativity but can come with unexpected results. Whenever a decision is placed in your lap, consider the consequences to ensure you can handle what follows. Analyze the "what if" questions as you brainstorm. Research situations and try to find best practices related to the decision you must address.

The steps to critical thinking include identifying the problem, fact gathering, and data analyzation. If working with a group, you should address any assumptions about the issue. Discuss the situation with viable solutions and prepare to communicate your decision or outcome.

Critical thinking skills become flawed when there is an intent to achieve a negative outcome. People with skewed thoughts and a hidden agenda will provide feedback that may not make sense or align with the target. Pay attention to selfish or insensitive comments. Such people will not reason effectively, will distort the truth, become irrational, and present as closed-minded individuals. They may call themselves a realist. The truth is these people do not want to hear what you have to say, thus; proceed with caution and evaluate the feedback accordingly.

How can you improve your critical thinking skills?

_____

_____

_____

T

Train others.

Serve as a mentor to others and teach them what you know. Most people will thank you for the shared knowledge and remember you in their retirement speech or in a book they might write. Develop others regardless of the unknown; some people fear that the person they train will take their position. If you happen to get replaced by someone new on your job, do not look at the situation as a setback. View this situation as an opportunity to move on to bigger things.

If you find yourself in a position that is less than desirable or where you think you should be, do your best and keep it moving. Get what you can out of the situation and try not to stress over it. Things happen for a reason and sometimes we cannot seem to figure out the "why" in life. During these times, the Lord positions you out of trouble or in the direction to help others. Stay grounded, keep it moving and allow nothing to interfere with accomplishing your goals.

Train as many people as you can; but if you can teach only one person something new once a day, you have done an excellent job. There is no need to hold on to knowledge. If you were given the gift of writing, speaking, or leading others, share your gift whatever it is. Some people will never have the opportunities you were afforded. Therefore, if you can, help others by giving them something they may never otherwise receive.

Teaching people does not really require a certification. You can train persons in your field of expertise as they prepare to get the credentials they need to serve as a professional. People should not allow the lack of formal education to weigh them down. Many successful people dropped out or opted out of the higher education experience. Depending on your field of interest, you can receive higher learning on your own and from others willing to train you.

Make liars out of everyone who said you would never make it or you are too old to do anything. Remind yourself every day that it is never too late to begin anew. You will eventually reach your goal no matter how many times you were knocked down. Train someone, and train someone to train someone else. Someone or two will thank you later.

How can you serve as a mentor for others?

_____

_____

_____

E

Execute.

You can set goals all day long, but if you do not execute you are wasting time. To execute is to carry out your plan by setting realistic, measurable, and achievable goals. A thought comes to mind, and you think it is a promising idea, so you brainstorm and write it down. You share it with someone who shoots it down with laughter. Before getting upset, ask what is so funny. If he or she finds humor in your idea because there is a lack of belief in you, that might serve as a good time to execute.

If people laugh because they think your idea is ridiculous and not so much because they do not believe in you, have a conversation about why your idea is perceived absurd. People may not see your vision and you may not understand their logic, but if you believe in your heart that you can accomplish your dream - say less and simply go for it.

Being misunderstood is completely okay. People will doubt you but, "Do not be anxious about anything, but in everything by prayer and supplication with thanksgiving let your requests be made known to God" (Philippians 4:6). I cannot stress this enough: you must believe in yourself and put your faith and trust in the Lord or your higher power. If you do not believe in yourself, why should others?

As you develop on this path of success, aim for excellence, and get up when you fall. Speed bumps and obstacles are everywhere—you must know how to get around or over them. Remember **DYH – Do You Have** what it takes to exude competence, use veracious language, and live by notable standards? Sure, you do. Tell yourself you can, and you will.

Once you reach your goal, set a new target with a bigger challenge. With all things considered, goal setting should be a part of everyday life. Small achievements such as brushing your teeth are grounds for celebration. I say this because there are some mentally challenged people who struggle with daily activities, that most people take for granted. Celebrate the good in life as you execute and accomplish your goals, stay focused, and reward yourself accordingly.

What goals are you planning to execute?

_____

_____

_____

R

Reliable.

Are you the person people call on when they need something? If so, that is probably because you have a dependable spirit. Reliable people are those responsible adults who live by a core code of values. They want to win in life, they can be trusted, and they often perform at a level higher than the norm. People with this character trait are reputable and rooted in integrity.

Reliable people are generally driven by stability. They are usually financially secure, are often in good health or they at least go to the doctor when they should, and they do not view good habits as a chore. Such people realize that life may seem like a rat race, but in all actuality, they know that life is what you make of it.

Make yourself available for others, stay true to your words and take responsibility for your actions. Quickly acknowledge faults and right any wrongs to avoid complicated outcomes. Always remain dependable and know when to disengage. Rely on yourself to live as a person with true integrity. Live how you want to be remembered after God or your chosen higher power calls you home to eternity. Develop your inner HERO with

147

every breath you take. Stay fit, stay focused, and stay positive...the rest will fall into place.

How reliable are you?

_____

_____

_____

PART FOUR

Public Speaking Help for HEROES

Communication is a part of life. Conveying a message may be expressed in sign or body language, in braille/written communication, or verbally. Employees must speak directly with people unless they have a job as a blogger or some type of virtual position that requires minimal talking.

Jobs which may require less talking, such as a kennel attendant, a mechanic, or a driver will communicate through various means. A tractor trailer driver will pull up to a loading dock, unlock and secure the rear cab, digitally sign some forms, and return to the truck. The loader will place items on the back of the trailer and may signal that everything is good to go by the two thumbs up symbol, or maybe even through electronic measures. No words are expressed during this phase of a driver's job.

Symbols and images were used in ancient times as one of the first forms of communication. Ideograms were also used to determine location. Today, ideograms are widely used in buildings. When you see a cigarette with a red circle around it and a line going through it; such image sends a message to your brain to let you know smoking is not allowed. Symbols are used on roads to caution you of left or right turns. No matter how a message is delivered I honestly believe we can all agree that communication is a vital aspect of life.

A key to effective communication is making sure everyone understands. You can talk, talk,

talk, and people will hear you, but they may not really listen to your words. Giving out information is particularly important, but are you really getting through to people with simple dialogue? That is the question. The late Nelson Mandela, political leader, and president of South Africa from 1994 to 1999, once said, "If you talk to a man in a language he understands, that goes to his head. If you talk to him in his language that goes to his heart."

One should articulate with business acumen in a professional setting, but some people are truly benighted when it comes to this talent. Using good old-fashioned English, jot down your thoughts on public speaking and prepare to receive tips that will help you with an interview, a public speech, or everyday conversation. Speak well, speak from your heart, and always speak the truth.

What are your thoughts on public speaking?

_____

_____

_____

P

Practice.

Write out your speech and read it aloud to hear how you sound, practice in front of a mirror, or record a video of yourself. At some point in your existence, you will have to speak at your place of employment. Regardless of how you do it, communication and general conversation are basic requirements for business. Practicing what you will say can help.

If you must give a speech, be it impromptu or professional, you should at least know how you are going to deliver it. An impromptu speech is discourse articulated without thought; therefore, it is best to know your job or topic of discussion well enough to speak on it at a moment's notice. You may not know the answers to every question asked of you, but at least have the courage to say that you do not know, and you will get back to the person after you have researched the answer.

Prior to delivering a speech, mentally prepare for challenging inquiries and have a notepad or tablet handy to jot down follow-up questions. It is good practice to have someone take notes for you. Either way, good preparation is a good method to have. If you fail to plan your presentation you can probably plan on failing at the delivery of your dialogue.

What can you do to improve your communication style?

_____

_____

_____

U

Uhhh, uh, um.

"Uhm" should be avoided and the least word out of your mouth when speaking. If you do not know what to say or if you arrive at a point of hesitation while conversing, do the following: pause, take a few breaths, and keep the audience oblivious of your weakness, fear, or the look of being ill-prepared. There is no need to say: "I am not used to speaking in front of people," "I am not a good public speaker," or "I did not know I had to speak." In most cases the audience will not know how nervous you are if you control your breathing and mannerisms.

Additionally, rumbling through papers displays poor preparation. Always look the part, and better yet, arrive prepared. You should always introduce yourself, even if you know the audience, you just never know when a surprise visitor may be in the crowd. Break up an intense audience with an ice breaker. Ice breakers are fun especially when you talk about current trends such as the latest Amazon purchase or Tik Tok video. If it is not a casual environment, you can mention a current event, the weather, or the topic of discussion as an opening statement. Positive audience inclusion is a good method for capturing attention and invoking a feeling of ease.

Having a comfortable audience is important when you are pitching a new idea. Studies show that people are more inclined to believe in you when they find it comfortable to listen to you. Presidential elections are often impacted by speeches. How well someone can deliver a point can sway the audience or the vote. Knowing what to say and when to use certain language enhances the delivery of your message and affects the listener.

How can you speak more persuasively?

_____

_____

_____

B

Be proactive.

Being proactive will get your audience fired up if you present with an enthusiastic attitude that implies you are ready to accomplish your objectives. Making your audience wait for you can have a subpar look and may set the tone for the outcome. In cases of an emergency, have a backup plan where someone can fill in for you during your absence. This is necessary, especially if people pay to hear you speak.

Upon arrival, thank your team for covering for you, and you can either apologize to the audience who may not have known you were late (depending on how well your team covered), or you can walk on stage with confidence as if you are right on time. Emergencies happen, but proper planning is key.

Time is irreversible. You cannot get it back once it is lost. Respect it and make the best of each second. Adjust your life to get what you want and remember, "You can have it all. You just can't have it all at once" Oprah Winfrey.

How can you become more proactive?

_____

_____

_____

L

Like what you do.

Having passion about your position or subject of discussion allows for an easy delivery of talking points. Onlookers can see right through nervous jitters; therefore, move about with poise and confidence as you speak. Allow your words to flow naturally. There may come a time where you are expected to speak on a subject of profound disinterest. Depending on the type of briefing you give, it is best to leave your personal feelings or thoughts out of the speech.

Remain unbiased when reporting material unless you are required to sway listeners in a certain direction; when this is the case, speak with conviction, persuasion, and influence. If your job is to present material, regardless of how you feel about it, do your job, collect your check, and go home. If you are totally dead set against the talking points, you probably should re-evaluate the "why" in your position.

Aside from social media, reporters are often the first to bring information into this vast world of ours. Cable TV stations such as CNN, *Fox* and MSNBC increased their viewership over time, particularly during the start of the Covid-19 global pandemic, according to a Pew Research feature from July 13, 2021. Despite the fact that some news anchors are one-sided, people will listen to voices that speak in a language they are able to comprehend. The key here is to like your job and do it well for the good of the organization you represent.

What do you like most about your job?

_____

_____

_____

I

Inflection can set the tone.

If you begin your speech by getting straight to the point, you may be viewed as a person who is direct and unswerving. On the flip side, a different emotion occurs if you elongate your words such as when saying something like, 'goooooood morniiiiiing.' The tone you use will touch each person in a separate way and each situation will vary according to the audience.

If you are in a court of law, you will need to curtail your speech accordingly and use inflection as required. Raising your voice to say, "HE IS INNOCENT," presents credibility over a monotonous tone. Think before you speak and keep in mind who you are addressing.

Inflection in your speech can sometimes let people know what mood you are in or simply set the tone for the environment. In one of my communication courses that I attended while working for the Hershey Foods Corporation, I was given a little tip to smile when answering the phone, or to place a post it on the phone so that you can see the smiley face as soon as you pick up the receiver. This trick changes the tone of your words. At this very moment I want you to say hello with a smile on your face, even if you must force it, and then say it without a smile.

What did you notice when smiling and saying hello vs. your hello without the smile?

_____

_____

_____

C

Captivate your audience.

Fascinating facts or a catchphrase will get listeners involved. A chant or uplifting words to produce change and encourage productivity also works. Here are a few ideas to help captivate your audience: If you are in a large group setting you can tell one side of the room to stand up and say a phrase to the other side of the room. Make the phrase something relevant. For example, if the topic is about wearing a mask, you can tell one side of the room to stand up, face the people on the opposite side of the room and yell, "Wear the mask!" Then redirect your attention to the people who just received the wail and have them squawk back the same comment. Continue this roar by charging them to say it louder and with more emphasis and meaning. After about three bouts of screaming, settle the audience down and begin your presentation. Trust me when I say, this will motivate your group.

Depending on the type of meeting you conduct, here is another powerful catchphrase to taunt one another: "Get money. Get Money. GET MONEY! GET MONEY!! GET MONEY!!!" Start out with a normal tone and then take the verbal pitch higher and higher with force and determination. Move about the room while charging people up. If you have not reached this point with your public speaking skills, you can always play a lead-in song or theme music. Good audience motivation and participation will hype the crowd, fire them up, and get them ready to listen. Learn how to work your audience.

During virtual presentations you can share your screen with a movie clip to motivate the audience or pose that ice breaker question. Use words to get them involved and listening to you. The goal is to win the audience over and leave them eager to hear more of what you have to say.

What can you do to captivate your listeners?

_____

_____

_____

S

Speak words your listeners will remember.

Truth, facts, and kindness go over well. Research your material and quote your sources. Plagiarism is a violation of ethical standards in the academic world. Universities and academic institutions may have policies in place to prevent the act of using someone else's work as if it is your original material or data. Always give credit where it is due.

The late Maya Angelou, a civil rights activist, authoress and poet, said, "I've learned that people will forget what you said, people will forget what you did, but people will never forget how you made them feel." Feelings are brought on by words, pictures, and actions. Speak words your listeners will remember.

"Successful people will always have two things on their lips: silence and a smile." "Do not mix harsh words with your bad mood. You'll have many opportunities to change your mood, but you'll never get the opportunity to replace the words you spoke" Buddha.

Use appropriate language: sexist statements should be left unspoken. Use clichés with caution due to potential misrepresentation of words and meanings. Leave the group with a thought-provoking quote or rhetorical question before you end your speech. Thank your audience for their time and attention and exit as powerful as you entered.

Reflect on a few memorable speeches that have impacted you.

_____

_____

_____

P

Points of discussion.

When giving a speech it is best to have talking points. Points of discussion can be written on a note card and used when you need to remember and refer to specific issues. This may be old school, but it still works, and I find it better than holding an electronic device such as a tablet in your hand to refer to your key points. Not only that, but an electronic device might also just stop working. Knowing the talking points ahead of time is ideal; this is where practice comes into place. Stick to your topics and align your main points to flawlessly transition as if story telling.

Avoid jumping around during your discussion and introducing new topics that were not a part of the original conversation. When your points of speech are scattered and disorganized the attention span of your audience decreases tremendously. People will pick up their phone, even if you have already asked them to place their phone on silent. There is always one person waiting on an important phone call, or the parent who will not put down their phone because they are virtually babysitting their children or watching a pet.

Stay focused on your subject, remember to pause if you get off track and allow the audience to sit in brief silence as you casually refer to your points of discussion. Using your phone to read notes should be done as a last resort. Perception is reality, and you may get accused of using or playing with your cellphone while speaking, if you use it to refer to your notes.

Lastly, stay on track with the allotted time for your presentation. If you have thirty minutes to speak, you can discreetly place a silent timer on the podium, or you can have someone strategically positioned to alert you of your pace. The time watcher should not be a part of your intended audience. You should avoid using your wristwatch to stay on point because it sends a misleading message to your group. People may think you have somewhere more important to be if you constantly look at your watch.

How do you remain on track when giving a speech?

_____

_____

_____

E

Eye contact.

Eye contact is often a challenge to maintain when you are in front of a crowd or even one-on-one with a person. This is one of the greatest tips you will want to remember. When you are engaged in a face-to-face conversation with someone, you probably should look the person straight in the eyes; or you can simply look at the person's eyebrows. This technique will take the pressure off staring into the soul of an individual. You can also look in between their eyes or at the person's forehead.

As you do this and face others while speaking, you may notice the other person looking away to avoid what they perceive as direct eye contact. Consider every eye contact encounter carefully, as some people and cultures may find it rude and may become uncomfortable if they feel as if you are staring.

Give audience/gatherings direct eye contact by peering over their heads. Look to the left corner of the room, scan above the heads in the center of the room and then make your way over to the right corner. Doing this will appear as if you have made eye contact with everyone in the room.

If standing in front of a group, simply move about from left to right. Avoid hugging the podium, meaning do not stand behind the podium the entire time. As you scan the room from left to right and then again from right to left, occasionally stop in front of someone and peer down at them while speaking. As you move about the room, remain front faced. If your back is facing them while you are talking, you have just *turned your back on them.*

During virtual meetings, it is best to have your camera on while speaking if you are the one facilitating. Determining if you want your virtual audience to turn on the cameras or not is your choice. Ask yourself if it is necessary to have persons turn on their camera. In some cases, the camera may need to be on in situations where you must give a virtual oath or legal proceedings. If you have dual screens you may appear to be looking away from everyone if your camera is angled. Most people will know that you have another screen, but some may not. When your camera is at an angle, you should occasionally look into the camera to connect with your virtual audience.

How can you improve eye contact and connection with others?

_____

_____

_____

A

Added distractions.

Added distractions during a speech can wreak havoc on a presentation. Announce the protocol of the briefing session before you start. After your introduction and after smoothing the path for discussion, it is best to announce administrative notes such as, the location of the bathroom and/or cell phone use.

Some people take serious offense to the words, 'please turn off your cell phones.' The sound of a vibrating phone can disturb others, so make sure you have this under control. Thus, state the etiquette for exiting the room in the event someone has an emergency. Almost always, there is one person with a pressing situation that requires him or her to step out.

Informing your audience of when a break will occur can ease the anticipation of folks wanting to get up and walk out. People like to know when a breather will come so they can stretch their legs, get some fresh air, or even take a smoke. Consider the audience and watch their behavior.

Spinoff conversations can distract the speaker from getting points across and it prevents others from hearing every word. As the presenter and controller of the room, it is wise to set the tone of the briefing by telling the group to take notes and when a question-and-answer period will occur.

I noticed throughout my employment history, there is always *ONE* - one person who will speak out of turn, one person who will walk out in the middle of a pivotal moment, and that one person who may act as if he or she is in control of the room and will do whatever he or she wants. When this occurs, keep mental health in mind.

Some folks find it difficult to sit for an extended period; even five minutes is a challenge. The best way to handle this is to have assistance in the room when possible or a person in the virtual chat who can communicate with everyone or individually as needed. Have the interruptions handled, or if you must take an unscheduled break do so and address the concerns with discretion.

How do you handle distractions?

_____

_____

_____

K

Know when to speak.

A good speaker can hold the listener's attention, while a more experienced speaker knows when to speak and when to pause. Remember that the attention span of an audience drifts after so many minutes and continues to dwindle the longer you talk. Speak with excitement and intensity to keep people tuned into your discussion. Grip the audience with your words. Over time, you want to develop the ability to speak in a manner that will impact or inform others.

Depending on your age, you may remember a commercial about EF Hutton. To give you a little background, EF Hutton is a financial services organization founded by Edward Francis Hutton and his brother Franklyn. This brokerage firm connects people with investments and solutions in areas such as taxes, real estate, and bonds. The notable phrase from the commercial was, "When EF Hutton talks, people listen." The advertisement depicted EF Hutton's name being mentioned during dinner at a restaurant or during a marching band. No matter the location, everything stopped, and people tuned in to hear the financial advice of EF Hutton.

Granted we may not be descendants of EF Hutton, but my point is to speak so people will listen. Know when to pause and ask open-ended questions that will promote active audience engagement.

Initially speak for about thirty or forty-five minutes then offer an intermission, as required, or requested. This break will allow you time to regroup if you happen to venture off track. When venturing off track, avoid mumbling or fumbling with anything. It is okay to allow folks to briefly sit calmly while you breathe deeply, gather your thoughts, and continue to blow them away with a graceful delivery.

Reflect on your last speech or conversation. How can you improve?

_____

_____

_____

I

Impromptu.

An impromptu speech is a presentation that you must give with or without minimal notice. This type of speech can cause complete anxiety. For example, you show up for work and the boss tells you that you must brief the new chief executive officer (CEO) on your department's operation and statistics. You wonder why the boss cannot conduct the briefing, but you really do not want to ask that one question a lot of leaders hate, and that is - WHY? So, you gingerly phrase your question to the boss and ask, "what is going on?" or "when was this scheduled?" The boss tells you that it was unscheduled; it just came up five minutes ago...along with an unexpected appointment the boss has, which is why he or she cannot meet with the CEO.

Now that the anxiety has caved in and the reality has hit you in the face, you can do several things. You can speak highly of the department and make everything sound great. You can also use this opportunity to tell the senior leader just how bad things are going in the office with hopes for a change and not retaliation (I don't recommend this, but I saw it happen). Lastly, you can just smile, introduce yourself, state the

175

mission of your department and where your department stands with accomplishing goals.

After your brief overview of the office, you can shift the attention to co-workers, so they, too, can meet the new CEO. Hopefully, only a few questions will go back and forth. This is a small example, but if you embrace the unknown with full confidence you should succeed. Tell yourself you can do it. Positive thoughts and an unshakable presence of mind will leave people wishing they too could speak with such intestinal fortitude.

What is your experience with impromptu speeches?

_____

_____

_____

N

Nonverbal cues.

Nonverbal cues are words unspoken. This language presents as time or clock watchers, yawns, or people who do an antsy chair dance. Such warnings should not be ignored. These loud indicators often serve as feedback as to how you are doing as the speaker. If as an adult you have a nonverbal learning disorder (NLD), you should speak with your doctor about how to treat this condition. If your supervisor is aware of your medical condition, request a reasonable accommodation that will aid in your performance and participation.

Employees with NLD can request a mentor on the job, have information written down, or use whatever method available to assist with comprehension of what is to be expected. Nonverbal picture boards are helpful, such as a cellphone inside a circle with a line going through it to imply that cellphones should not be used. The NLD employee can use a sheet with multiple cues listed on the chart to indicate what should not occur while speaking.

When possible, solicit a written or online assessment of your commentary and use the evaluations to improve your next lecture. As you prepare for your next speech, think about commanding the room without words. A powerful leader will possess command presence just by walking in the room and standing there. Nothing needs to be said. Folks may end up clapping just by the mere sight of a renowned speaker. The chatter will stop, the focus is attentive, and all eyes are fixated on the first spoken word.

How do you adjust to nonverbal cues?

_____

_____

_____

G

Get your message to the back of the room.

Project your voice as if talking to the rear wall. There is no need to yell or shout; just strive for audible delivery. When in doubt, use a microphone or ask the audience if they can hear you. Clearly speak as if having a conversation with a large group of people. Make it casual, comfortable, and delivered with confidence. Use inflection to emphasize main points because a monotone voice can cause people to fall asleep or prompt disinterest.

Speeches are given for distinct reasons such as to persuade, serve as a sales pitch, or to inform. Regardless of the reason, be understood professionally when you need to deliver a message with good order especially when voice apps are a click away. What you say can be taken out of context and misconstrued across social media.

In a recent conversation with someone who wanted to interview me, I was asked a few questions and I began spewing my personal feelings about a situation. Speaking passionately about something is okay, just be careful about your emotional expressions. Nonetheless, this person asked if they could step away to write down their questions for the interview, I said, "sure."

Upon her return with pen and notepad, the interviewer stated that her phone automatically recorded me. She asked if she could use the content for a part of her story. I was surprised at her casual expression when she told me the app on her phone picked up my voice. She acted as if this was normal as she stated that people record others all the time. I agreed with her and then asked if she thought it was okay to record someone without their knowledge.

Apparently, this person thought this was an innocent act, even though she knew she had the app on her phone, and she knew how it worked. She never apologized, yet asked if she could continue. As awkward as this moment was, I asked her to think about her integrity and character. I told her to delete the initial conversation and to start over by asking me for permission to record the interview.

Be heard; be positively heard in the back of the room.

Reflect on your experience with voice projection.

_____

_____

_____

Finalé

Now that you have reached the back of this book, what are you going to do with yourself? Jim Rohn said, "If you really want to do something, you'll find a way. If you don't, you'll find an excuse."

I hope you have enjoyed this read. Please visit www.docupublishing.org and/or visit www.lulu.com and www.amazon.com to write a review, and share your takeaways.

May God bless you with a beautiful life and a fulfilling career.

Thank you!

About the Author

Darlise Y. Henderson is a retired Army Veteran, has traveled throughout the United States, and overseas in support of multiple humanitarian missions and training exercises.

She completed extensive military education and served in the human resources and medical field. She was awarded the Air Assault Badge while stationed at Fort Campbell, Kentucky where she deployed during the First Gulf war – Operation Desert Shield/Desert Storm.

Darlise received a master's degree in Public Relations from Liberty University. Prior to that she attended the University of Maryland Global Campus and earned her undergraduate degree in Management / Communications.

The Developing Young HEROES (DYH) youth and young adult (virtual and resident) leadership training program was implemented by Darlise following her retirement from the military. The DYH vision is designed to positively promote the common good and general welfare of our communities' rising generation.

As a level 2 Reiki Practitioner, Darlise spends her spare time meditating, exercising, and writing. She is the proud mother of Dionna and Ja'Ir.

Connect with the author—Email Darlise at relaxvet@gmail.com.

www.ingramcontent.com/pod-product-compliance
Lightning Source LLC
Chambersburg PA
CBHW070400200326
41518CB00011B/2008